BUILDING COMMUNICATION
NETWORKS WITH
DISTRIBUTED OBJECTS

THE McGRAW-HILL SERIES ON COMPUTER COMMUNICATIONS (SELECTED TITLES)

To order or receive additional information on these or any other McGraw-Hill titles, in the United States please call 1-800-722-4726. In other countries, contact your local McGraw-Hill representative.

Building Communication Networks with Distributed Objects

William J. Yarborough

McGraw-Hill
New York   San Francisco   Washington, D.C.
Auckland   Bogotá   Caracas   Lisbon   London
Madrid   Mexico City   Milan   Montreal
New Delhi   San Juan   Singapore   Sydney
Tokyo   Toronto

Library of Congress Cataloging-in-Publication Data

Yarborough, William J.
    Building communication networks with distributed
objects / William J. Yarborough.
        p.   cm.
    Includes index.
    ISBN 0-07-072220-X
    1. Client/server computing.   2. Object-oriented programming
(Computer science)   3. Electronic data processing—Distributed
processing.   4. Computer networks.   I. Title.
QA76.9.C55Y37   1998
004'.36—dc21   97-34673
                                                            CIP

McGraw-Hill

*A Division of The **McGraw·Hill** Companies*

1 2 3 4 5 6 7 8 9 0   DOC/DOC   9 0 2 1 0 9 8 7

ISBN 0-07-072220-X

The sponsoring editors for this book were Steven Elliot and John Wyzalek, the editing supervisor was Caroline R. Levine, and the production supervisor was Sherri Souffrance. It was set in Vendome by Don Feldman of McGraw-Hill's Professional Book Group composition unit.

Printed and bound by R. R. Donnelley & Sons Company.

McGraw-Hill books are available at special quantity discounts to use as premiums and sales promotions, or for use in corporate training programs. For more information, please write to the Director of Special Sales, McGraw-Hill, 11 West 19th Street, New York, NY 10011. Or contact your local bookstore.

 This book is printed on recycled, acid-free paper containing a minimum of 50% recycled, de-inked fiber.

CONTENTS

Contents

PREFACE

This book tells the story of the development and implementation of a network infrastructure to support distributed objects. Unlike other networking books, which focus in some detail on different layers of the network, such as frame relay, ISDN, TCP/IP, and the like, this book presents all layers of the network architecture without deep analysis of the internals of the various networking technologies, for which volumes already exist. An outline of the individual chapters follows:

CHAPTER 1. The objectives of the network implementation are presented, and a discussion of the client/server requirements is extended to include implementation challenges for network architects.

CHAPTER 2. An organizational hierarchy for the various components found on a network, along with many of the different products available, is presented. This chapter provides a most useful framework in which to think about network architecture.

CHAPTER 3. LAN and WAN technologies, along with different network topologies that commonly support client/server computing, are discussed.

CHAPTER 4. This chapter presents software services, including different network protocols such as TCP/IP, and SNA APPN, Netbios, and Netware.

CHAPTER 5. Various middleware types and a discussion of certain example implementations such as DCE, Sybase open server/open client, and MQ series, are presented.

CHAPTER 6. A short chapter on network application addresses.

CHAPTER 7. Network security, implementation of proxy services, and how they work with TCP/IP and remote access are discussed.

CHAPTER 8. This chapter presents the topology of the Internet and ways it can be used to support remote customer access.

CHAPTER 9. A detailed architecture of MVS SNA/TCP/IP gateways and the team needed to build one are provided.

CHAPTER 10. This chapter provides an example network implementation and includes application Gateway, SNA configurations for Link, session, and conversation connectivity.

CHAPTER 11. Different communication models, including synchronous versus asynchronous and peer-to-peer versus client/server, are examined. The C++ code is presented to implement a concurrent single multiplexed sockets server.

CHAPTER 12. A class to implement SNA LU6.2 connections is discussed, and a C++ SNA class is presented.

CHAPTER 13. This chapter builds an application using the classes developed in Chaps. 11 and 12.

CHAPTER 14. A multiprocess concurrent server, along with the logic used to implement it, is discussed.

CHAPTER 15. The code for the multiprocess concurrent server is presented.

This book is not an easy read; the material presented is extensive. However, it will provide the reader with an understanding of the use of different network technologies to support distributed objects. Any questions or comments are invited to my e-mail address: **infoalt@ao1.com.**

—WILLIAM J. YARBOROUGH

1

Network Strategy

Many years ago, large corporations realized the value of providing customers with direct access to internal proprietary computer systems. Customer response times were shortened, paperwork was reduced, and customer service activities were refocused toward system support. Customer satisfaction increased, and manual processes were reduced. It was a win-win phenomenon that gave birth to some significant new products and business, such as home banking and value-added networks.

Until quite recently, these services were provided by remote terminal access, such as TTY or 3270 emulation, or by file transfers, which evolved from RJE-type protocols to modern, more effective products such as NDM or XCOM. With the advent and proliferation of PCs, we began to write DOS and then Windows applications for the customer's desktop, but when communication with the corporate host was required, we usually reverted to terminal emulation, shielding it from the end-user wherever possible.

When LANs became prevalent at corporate headquarters and we began to deploy critical business systems off the mainframe, we realized that we needed to make these resources available remotely. But we concentrated our efforts on corporate employees, supporting the traveling salesperson and the weekend workaholic.

New communications products, both hardware and software, were developed and marketed, but the focus was on single-node-to-network connectivity with employees as end-users.

Today, we realize the opportunities and challenges of extending our distributed systems and network services to our clients. The explosive growth of the Internet and the growing business need for more data, more functionality, and greater timeliness has made it imperative for businesses to explore this direction.

This chapter discusses seven elements that corporate networks must provide end-users if they are to compete in this new world and reviews briefly the emergence of client/server enabling technology (see Fig. 1.1).

Elements of Corporate Networks

Transparent Data Location

Arguably, transparent data location is the primary force driving the development of data networks to support client/server computing. The application layer at the client workstation must be able to execute a variety of data management commands without knowledge of data location, database or file type, operating system, network protocols, or platform location.

With this, client views of the business can be constructed to meet the business requirement and give the user a concise answer to the questions he or she may ask. The development of the network architecture to support this one requirement requires extensive analysis and examina-

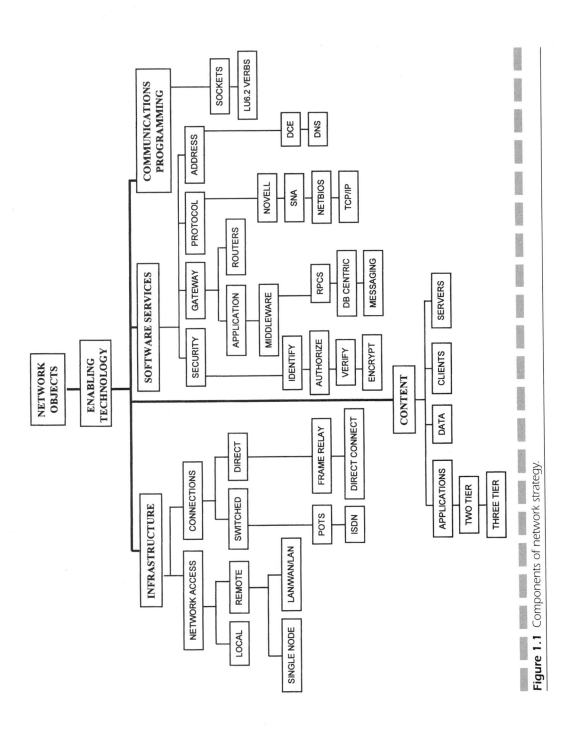

Figure 1.1 Components of network strategy.

3

tion. The other six goals in some ways can be thought of as subsets of this one requirement.

Security Commensurate with Corporate Policy

With the evolution of client/server technology and the underlying enabling network technology, network plants have been extended across various geographical locations to form interconnected networks with remote access availability.

With the advancement of switched dial-up connections like 28.8-kbps POTS (plain old telephone service) and even faster 128-kbps ISDN (integrated services digital network), the demand for dial-up access has increased substantially. The combination of corporations offering data access to customers and remote node extensions to the network has made corporate data resources far more vulnerable to unauthorized access than ever before.

The corporate security forces responsible for protecting these resources have imposed a number of security requirements. Users, on the other hand, have demanded a simple method for accessing their data on the corporate LAN. These two goals often come into conflict. However, through an analysis of the requirements of each, and a review of the newest security products, combined with controlled access to the corporate data network, both criteria can be met.

Optimum Distribution of Data and Function

Along with the requirements of data access and network security comes the requirement to deliver these functions in a timely manner. The development and distribution of application network services often require that user databases be placed and distributed on a variety of platforms. Application services, often composed of a number of programs, objects, or functions, may also be distributed over different nodes and transparently available as services. These include the application security services, addressing services, formatting service, and database services. Today's networks must support a variety of application architectures. These designs are often expressed as two- and three-tier implementations.

N-Tier Technology

The development of two- and three-tier application technology services has evolved to support methods of optimally placing data and function across the network. These *N*-tier services allow business rules, security processes, application services, and database access services to exist in distributed pieces across the network infrastructure. The placement of these services is often over different network technologies, on different platforms, and in different databases. The data transparency, transparent security, and optimum distribution of data and function are all required in order to support *N*-tier technologies.

Internet-friendly

In today's interconnected world, the power of the public Internet can hardly be ignored. At the same time, the risks presented by this technology must be considered. Just as Internet technology now extends local access to worldwide clients and servers over a network of networks, the same interconnectivity increases the risk to corporate data resources connected to the public Internet.

At the same time, the rising popularity of the World Wide Web (WWW) and the enabling Hypertext Transport Protocol (HTTP) servers offer tremendous potential to corporations providing services over an existing network infrastructure. For example, the optimum distribution of data and function may include the use of HTTP servers enabled with interfaces to back-end databases for user data store access.

These two Internet resources, the WWW and the use of existing local network connections, make it possible for corporations to provide user access to data stores in an economic manner, by reducing development and maintenance costs.

Since the application-layer code exists in the Hypertext Markup Language (HTML), commercial browsers are purchased to view the HTML pages encoded by HTTP servers. No client code need be developed or maintained. Likewise, secure HTTP servers used by commercially available clients can now be purchased and deployed.

These technologies, which are still in their infancy, will soon host a variety of other services, including videoconferencing. New and personal ways of connecting to and servicing potential customers will ultimately be an everyday offering on Internet platforms and networks.

Supporting different technologies which enable a variety of bandwidth technologies is a key component of any network infrastructure. As such, multiple connectivity options which provide different bandwidths can enable a variety of applications and user requirements.

Multiple Connectivity Options

Enabling application services, and at the same time limiting them, is the availability of bandwidth to the application client. It is here that the physical- and link-layer connectivity mediums actually provide the application client with the roadway to the application servers. Just how fast data can travel over the roadway often determines the types of services available and how satisfied a particular network user is.

The ability to provide users with different connectivity options ensures that users may access the network using different bandwidths, but are at the same time able to upgrade the bandwidth as the application services require, technology enables, and economics permit. These different options include everything from 28.8-kbps modems to ISDN services and direct-connect frame relay.

Redundant Firewalled Proxy Services

Proxy services on firewalled external LANs are a means of providing security, data transparency, and optimum distribution of data and function. Proxy services are so important in client/server design, especially for remotely located customers, that this becomes a critical software service. Using proxy services as a point of access for remote users, a gateway is developed through which these proxy services can route application requests to the appropriate servers.

These services exist on the gateway and act as both application proxy agents and protocol converters, if needed. Their IP addresses and port numbers are well known to all clients needing these services. Likewise, these port numbers and IP addresses can be placed in Domain Name Services (DNS) servers. The client may then call the DNS server to find the address of the proxy service available to it.

Additionally, network security is enhanced through a single point of access. Once users locate the proxy service needed on the gateway, the client requests permission to connect to that service by contacting a security service. For example, a client requesting permission to get data from an LU6.2 mainframe service on the gateway would connect to a gateway proxy service, then send a user ID and password.

When the proxy LU6.2 service receives the request, it asks the security server to validate the login and password as those of a legitimate user of this service. Once the login and password are validated, the security server issues a token good for that session. The token is returned to both the application and the client. Any additional messages received by that service must contain the token; otherwise, the message is not considered to have originated from a valid user.

Additionally, these single-point-of-access gateways provide excellent value as a single place at which to log all user requests, and a single point at which to place monitoring software to detect unwanted intrusions.

Emergence of Enabling Client/Server Network Technology

Popular WAN protocols like X.25, while useful for connecting enterprise-wide WANs or remote LANs to each other, did not address the issues of application-to-application connectivity. X.25 was meant to address networking issues on wide-area networks, not on the local networks where most business application programs resided.

Other developments, like the emergence of standards for LAN-based networks, allowed communication between the different pieces of the application in a standard manner (Fig. 1.2). In fact, the OSI seven-layer model addresses the preferred way in which networking vendors should provide connectivity. The adoption of these standards, and their use by different software vendors, made it possible for client/server technology to exist and coexist. Published interface standards that established protocols for different layers in the OSI model emerged. And when examination of TCP/IP network protocols compared favorably with the OSI model, this public domain networking software soon began to see a host of vendors building their products to ride on top of it.

The protocol stacks diagram (Fig. 1.3) shows the various layers of the OSI architecture, and compares the TCP/IP protocol stack to it. While TCP and IP addressed only two of the seven layers of the OSI network architecture (network and transport), TCP/IP became the glue that other competing vendors could agree on and build their products (both above and below the two layers) to support. These included vendors who

8

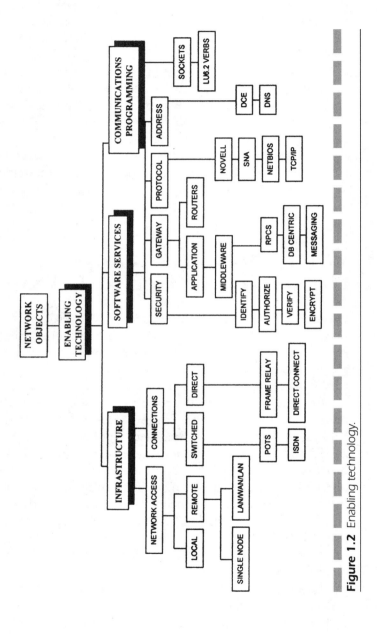

Figure 1.2 Enabling technology.

Figure 1.3
Protocol stacks.

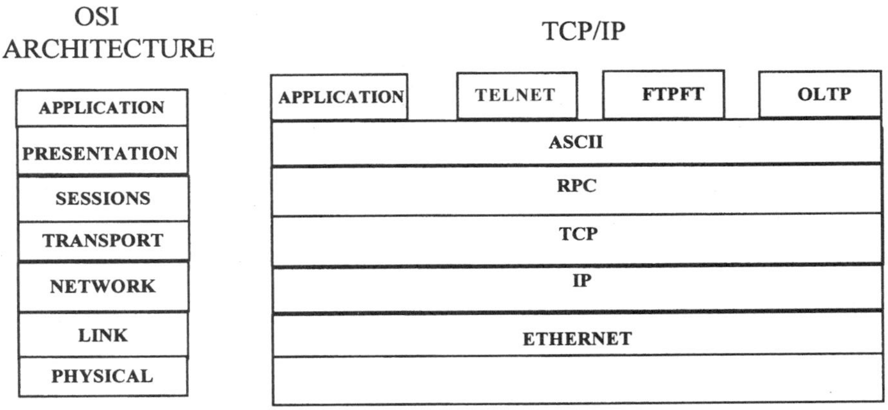

OSI ARCHITECTURE
APPLICATION
PRESENTATION
SESSIONS
TRANSPORT
NETWORK
LINK
PHYSICAL

TCP/IP

APPLICATION	TELNET	FTPFT	OLTP
ASCII			
RPC			
TCP			
IP			
ETHERNET			

had their own products to sell and an embedded customer base to support.

For example, lower-layer LAN protocols like Ethernet and token ring technologies, while they addressed connectivity between platforms, had no enabling software to address connectivity between programs running on these platforms (Netbios provided token ring users with hardware-addressable solutions). And while these link-layer and physical-layer protocols were useful on their own networks, there was no overall consensus on how to manage enterprise-wide networks that used both token ring and Ethernet technologies. Since these enterprise-wide networks were made up of many smaller LANs, TCP/IP addressed such issues as ways to route requests not on one LAN but between different LANs.

Network Integration Issues

The OSI seven-layer model, though meant as a guide for the development of future networking software, has as one end objective the support of end-user computing by providing a network to support the development and maintenance of network computing.

The resolution of network integration issues to support network computing was facilitated by applying the basic OSI model and standards to the different technologies existing in today's corporate data networks. Therefore, the model is presented briefly.

OSI

The OSI provides three types of standards.

- The first standard is intrinsic in the seven-layer model itself and defines the broad components of a network computing environment.
- The second standard depicts what each of these layers must do to support the layer above it.
- The third standard depicts how each layer will relate to the layer above it.

By context, then, the model starts with the physical layer of the network and stacks each layer to produce the requirements for network computing within a homogeneous protocol environment. Each layer represents an additional layer of interconnectivity between platform nodes, until full interoperability is achieved at the seventh layer (application-to-application connectivity).

Rather than representing any particular solutions, the protocol model presents requirements for solutions and is a useful guide by which to judge particular network protocol implementations and understand certain enabling technologies.

TCP/IP and OSI

For example, TCP represents the transport layer (layer 4) and IP the network layer (layer 3). The Ethernet protocol, token ring technology, and SDLC represent layer 2 or link-layer protocols. Implementations of these existing technologies are not necessarily independent of the layer above, and disparity between the implementations increases the higher up the protocol stack you go. However, the OSI layers provide an excellent way to judge the degree of functionality provided on the network and what must be done to achieve full network application computing.

For example, TCP/IP allows sessions to be established between software on network nodes. In analogous terms, that means that a telephone call can be placed between the two platforms. The user must still manage the sessions and the conversations that occur over them. RPCs (Remote Procedure Calls) provide the session-level management, and represent layer 5 of the architecture. This is close to application-to-application, but that is not achieved until layer 6, where presentation issues are addressed.

When the network layers are all represented by interoperable products, network computing between platforms hosting these same protocol stacks can be supported.

Unfortunately, things are not always so convenient. Many corporate computing environments host different protocol stacks. Even though each one may represent the seven-layer functionality required for network computing, they don't do it in the same way. Hence, different protocol stacks are not interoperable. Examples are shown in Fig. 1.4.

To achieve network computing, integration between the different protocol stacks is required. Such integration is enabled by protocol gateways to translate between the different protocol stacks. Examples of these include Netbios to TCP/IP, Novell to TCP/IP, and TCP/IP to SNA.

Such gateways provide programming interfaces used by application programs to allow a program on one network node serviced by one protocol stack to talk to another program on another network node serviced by another protocol stack. For example, a C program running in a UNIX environment needs to exchange data directly with a COBOL program running in an MVS environment. At this point, a network computing environment is established and data can flow over the network between the programs resident on the different platforms.

These talking applications use the LU6.2 protocol guidelines developed by IBM to support peer-to-peer processing, and this standard has become the primary method for developing internetwork application computing.

Once connectivity is established between the different network protocols, it is possible to support distributed computing and cooperative processing between the network environments. This does not mean that

Figure 1.4
Network integration.

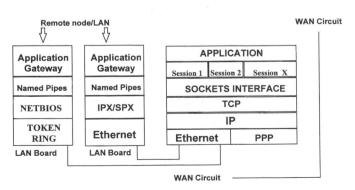

there are any business applications running. Business applications take various forms, but generally involve moving data from database to desktop and from desktop to database. Implementation strategies to achieve this generally take two forms: file transfer or on-demand transaction processing.

There are a host of issues involved in the development of distributed databases and cooperative processing technology, but it is enough to say at this point that they are not relevant unless the enabling technology to support application-to-application connectivity exists.

Although Novell networks, Netbios, and SNA have their share of the market, TCP/IP has clearly emerged as the standard for client/server. And Netbios running over TCP/IP as well as Novell gateways that convert Novell to TCP/IP are emerging, proving that TCP/IP has in fact become the de facto client/server standard on the LAN.

The development of Open Data Base Calls (ODBC) and the integration of this technology on top of many networking protocols like TCP, Novell, and Netbios gives further impetus to two-tier database applications.

When ODBC interfaces were introduced into Windows, the networking software became hidden from the applications developer. Client programs written in Visual Basic and other graphical user interface (GUI) languages were able to make calls to the ODBC interface. This interface, in turn, made calls to the transport layer through vendor-supplied files. These transport layers, while often TCP, could also be Novell and Netbios. Communication libraries handled all the network connections between the presentation client and the database server. Figure 1.5 illustrates a typical architecture.

To be sure, these early efforts at transparent retrieval and update of data between a client machine and a database server over a common network were and are not without problems. While easy to develop, these applications with presentation systems directly accessing a database server did not scale well. In other words, these types of systems were useful only for small groups. Larger groups of users doing simultaneous database access resulted in dismal performance.

Figure 1.5
Windows workstation architecture.

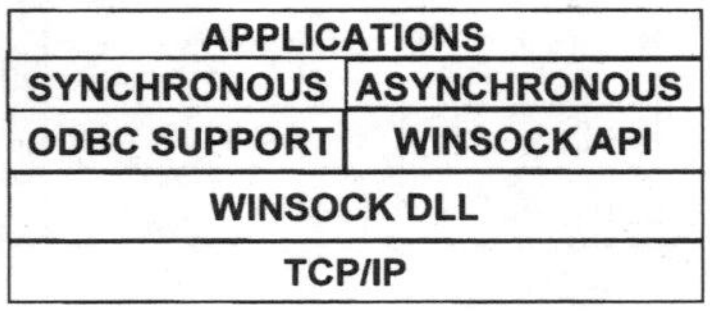

APPLICATIONS	
SYNCHRONOUS	ASYNCHRONOUS
ODBC SUPPORT	WINSOCK API
WINSOCK DLL	
TCP/IP	

Exacerbating the performance problem, these new database tools enabled users to construct their own queries. These ad hoc database queries and access were in no way optimized; since they were unpredictable, they often tied up a database server for inordinately long search times. These challenges are still being met and overcome in today's development market. In fact, from these early two-tier systems, which often employ both the business and processing rules on the client desktop, a whole new range of design alternatives have been developed, along with, as usual, a whole new list of buzzwords.

2

Network Structure

This chapter introduces the reader to the computer network. It provides an overview of the different components used in providing connectivity to applications. The diagrams in this chapter show the content and organization of the book. The reader may view them as object classes from which different instances are derived in the form of specific technologies, or simply as a classification of the different network components and technologies used on a network.

Network Components

Viewing the different components of the network as classes and the various technologies as instances of those classes facilitates the idea of "building networks to support distributed objects." However, an understanding of classes and objects is not necessary in order to understand the various components of a network presented in the first 10 chapters of this book.

It is not until Chap. 11, "Communications Programming," that C++ and software development object technology are discussed.

Modern corporate networks involve a variety of equipment and software from different vendors which must be made to work together to support client/server applications. This book lays out a strategy for providing that integration. Illustrated in Fig. 2.1 is a high-level diagram of the various generic components found on a network and two example occurrences of a network, the public Internet and a private intranet. As the figure shows, enabling technology and content are the two categories from which all the others are derived.

Enabling Technology and Content

In this instance the content of the network—applications, databases, client platforms, and server platforms—uses the enabling technology components to communicate. This book concentrates on the enabling technology needed to support communication among the members of the content class. Examples of network objects like the public Internet and private intranets and their enabling technology are also discussed.

Figure 2.1
Example occurrences of a network: the public Internet and a private intranet.

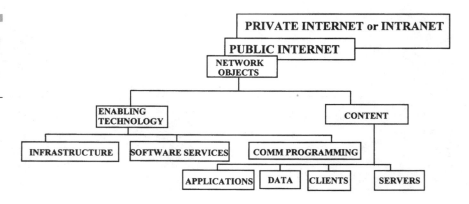

Although applications consist of two or three tiers, this book concerns itself more with the implications of such design for infrastructure.

Under *enabling technology* are *infrastructure, software services,* and *communications programming.* And as shown in Fig. 2.2, the infrastructure is further subdivided into *network access* and *connections.* Network access deals with the manner in which users or clients access services. This is further defined as either local access on the LAN or remote access.

Note that network access uses connections to satisfy local access and remote access. For example, connections are considered to be either switched or direct. And these are further subdivided into actual objects. The switched objects consist of ISDN (integrated services digital network) services or POTS (plain old telephone service). The direct connections contain frame relay or point-to-point leased lines and Ethernet or token ring adaptors.

Local connections use the direct connection objects like token ring or Ethernet to provide network access for members of the content class, which consist of applications, among other things.

Remote node classes are divided into two additional subclasses, *single node* and *LAN/WAN/LAN.* Remote node connections are satisfied with switched or direct connections to provide network access for content classes. These switched connections are via POTS or ISDN objects. The WAN connections are either frame relay or direct leased line between Ethernet or token ring connections.

Figure 2.3 details the software services subclass of enabling technology. It contains the software and services that the content class uses on the network to enable applications and data access over client/server nodes. This subclass is further subdivided into *security, gateway,* and *protocol* classes.

Figure 2.2
Enabling technology
components.

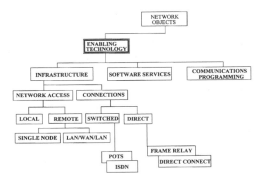

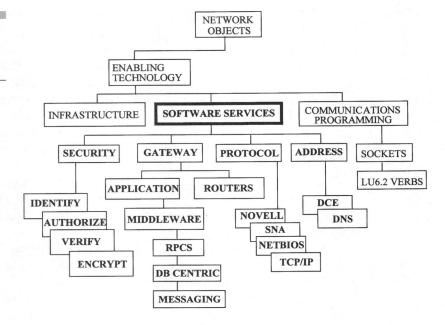

Software services classes actually use the infrastructure class objects to provide their services to the content class. For example, clients and servers gain access to the network through infrastructure objects like ISDN, frame relay, Ethernet, or token ring, but applications often need security services and gateways (routers and application gateways) to permit data access.

Furthermore, client applications need addressing services to provide location information for the server applications they may be trying to access. These addressing services include DNS (Domain Name Services) and DCE (Distributed Computing Environment) Directory Services.

Network software services are composed of various network protocols, middleware, and enabling software which sit below the application but give the application access to the various resources, data, and other application services on the network.

Additionally, DNS and DCE services are included in this category. Other software infrastructure objects include security services. Arguably, Hypertext Transport Protocol (HTTP) servers are software infrastructure service components.

Communications Programming

The third category, communications programming, refers to the inter-faces needed by clients and servers if they are to talk to the network resources. Sometimes these are provided with the middleware products; other times, middleware is not used, and these products act on behalf of the client and server applications to enable communication between the applications.

There are many different types of communication programming interfaces. These interfaces are provided by the network protocol and used by communication programs. The two most commonly used today are socket calls, which enable transport over TCP and Novell's SPX, and LU6.2 verbs for peer-to-peer processing over SNA networks. LU6.2 has been ported for use over TCP/IP as well.

Distributed vs. Single Applications

When applications ran as one piece on a mainframe, accessed by termi-nals, networking issues, while significant, were not paramount. And cer-tainly the applications programmer and the systems analyst were not concerned with network technology. Post-client/server, networking issues were usually reserved for the technician, who occasionally made an appearance if there was something wrong with a terminal. Because networks were accessed via terminals and used to display output or pro-vide input for programs running in a central location, there wasn't much association between an application and the data communications (see "Centralized Applications" in Fig. 2.5). To be sure, there are still many such applications around, and they are still being developed.

Figure 2.4
Network content des-cription: distributed vs. single application.

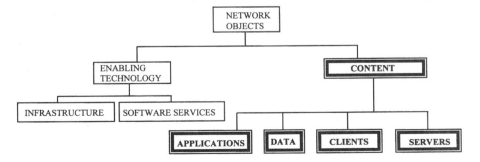

Figure 2.5
Centralized vs. distributed applications.

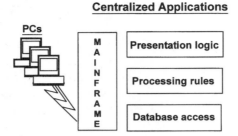

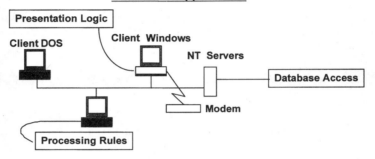

With the distribution of computer applications over several different platforms, the network technology used to communicate between the different parts of the application has taken on more significance, and the interfaces between the application and the network have created a new discipline altogether. These applications have provided users with a whole range of new possibilities. In fact, the presentation logic, while integrated with the rest of the application, is designed separately. The presentation layer is no longer dependent on the location of the particular data or database system (see "Distributed Applications" in Fig. 2.5).

To be sure, this freedom between presentation and database location provided tremendous new opportunities for value-added business processing. The database access logic became encapsulated in processing requirement modules which resided on separate, networked platforms.

This evolution from a single program containing the presentation, processing rules, and database access to independent and distributed applications has occurred concurrently with enabling network, platform, and software technologies.

From an engineering perspective, the biggest change brought about by distributed applications has been in the application architecture. The architecture has, of course, come to refer to three parts of an application: database, processing rules, and the presentation logic. Even the term *application architecture* itself is a new phenomenon.

With the change in thinking about business applications from centralized to distributed, distribution of the application created a whole new series of opportunities and issues.

Small computer systems networked together now provide business applications that were previously hosted on large computer systems. Moreover, user interfaces are engineered with a variety of added functionality that would have been impossible or too expensive using traditional host program interfaces. This includes all the Windows-based and Motif-based programming tools.

Servers

In addition to these various networking protocols, there are several prominent platform operating systems with which network protocols must ultimately interface to provide networking services to the existing application programs running on the server. The four most important are listed in Fig. 2.6.

Figure 2.6
Server and network examples.

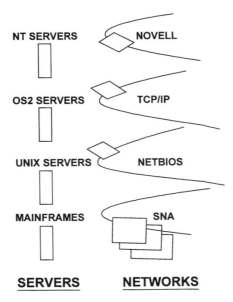

NT SERVERS   NOVELL

OS2 SERVERS   TCP/IP

UNIX SERVERS   NETBIOS

MAINFRAMES   SNA

SERVERS   **NETWORKS**

Although mainframes are typically SNA network members only, the other three—NT servers, OS/2 servers, and UNIX servers, including Sun, HP, IBM, AIX, and SCO—operate on all the networks listed.

Many of these servers are used as application gateway hosts between different networking protocols. The Novell network is a little different in this respect. It is important to distinguish between platform operating systems and network operating systems (NOS). Network operating systems usually provide hardware and software services to member nodes which host other operating systems like the ones mentioned.

As part of these implementations, redirectors send NOS commands to the server hosting the NOS. Local operating system commands get redirected to local systems. This is true for both Netbios and Novell. TCP/IP is different in this regard, however. TCP/IP is not a LAN operating system. It is a protocol suite.

As such, TCP/IP exists on the various nodes and interfaces with the different operating systems as a defined set of API calls used by the applications to access network resources. It has a network addressing scheme, independent routable packets, and guaranteed point-to-point delivery as well as a broadcast mechanism over member nodes.

The well-known sockets and transport-layer interface (TLI) calls are supported with the same application program interface (API) regardless of the operating system. That combined with the fact that TCP/IP is public domain software, is routable, and has extensions to it that include file transfer provisions, e-mail, and network management (SNMP) makes it a de facto standard in the computing world today.

The resource directory service, DNS, besides containing a list of every known computer on the network, also is useful as a means of locating the different networking services offered on those nodes. A complex product in and of itself, DNS is enabled by the TCP/IP protocol suite. DNS can thus be a useful tool to a network applications architect who is considering a scheme by which clients can identify and connect to a variety of network services located on different nodes on a network.

Clients

Just as there are different operating systems hosting servers, those same operating systems, such as Windows, DOS, and Windows 95, host a variety of application software. This software acts as clients and needs to request services from the network. Achieving this within the local LAN where the clients reside is less complicated than traversing multiple LANs.

Not only are there different flavors of clients which reside on Ethernet and token ring networks, there are stand-alone systems which connect over switched connections and request services from a network. This describes 90 percent of the clients on the Internet and also includes many remote node setups.

For all these different platforms, client programs must exist and network application interfaces (APIs) must be provided to enable these programs to request services. Additionally, addressing schemes for these services provide location information, and client addresses provide return addresses for the data requested. The value of TCP/IP is uniformity of the APIs on each of the clients and servers listed, the architected addressing scheme provided by IP nomenclature, and the usefulness of DNS in locating application services.

The complexity of connectivity requirements given the mix of different environments is shown in Fig. 2.7. Such tools as routers, application

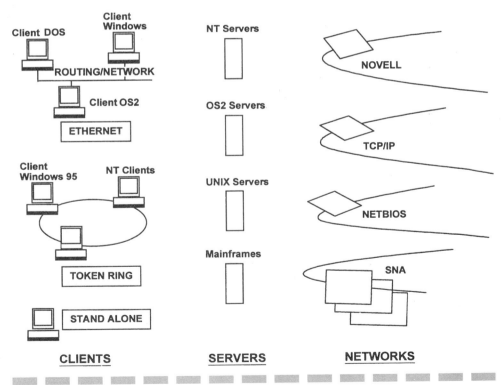

Figure 2.7 Clients, servers, and networks diagram.

gateways, protocol converters, and network encapsulation methods have been developed to enable this variety of networked environments to host application services.

These application services can be placed on a variety of platforms hosting different operating systems. Clients running on a number of platforms and different LAN types can use the network, connect to servers, and take advantage of these services.

Corporate Data

A variety of clients need to get to data located in different places on a corporate network (see Fig. 2.8). The data often resides in different vendor databases (such as Oracle and Sybase) and on different networks (like token ring and Ethernet), each of which may host different protocol stacks (notably SNA and TCP/IP), with platforms using different operating systems.

The requirement for transparent data access and optimum location of data and function is a difficult one in this environment. But the network must be architected with sufficient services to allow data access from client programs used to construct business views of the corporate data.

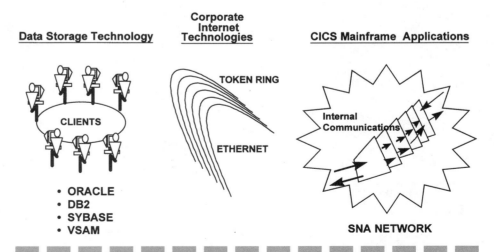

Figure 2.8 Data distribution in a corporate network environment.

By providing the needed number of different proxy services running on a gateway, clients can connect to these different environments. The different types of LANs, Ethernet and token ring, are connected through routers which bridge the difference between the protocols. And the use of a common protocol like TCP/IP on the LAN simplifies the location of and communication between the programs (clients and servers) running on the different networks.

Where common protocols aren't possible, application gateways are employed to bridge the conversation between the programs. If a single point of access is provided for remote users, the security issues can be addressed in one single place.

First Client/Server Applications

It wasn't long after personal computers began appearing on the business desktop that the economics of sharing expensive hardware like printers, disk space, and tape drivers among various PC users stimulated the development of local area networks (LANs). These early efforts produced the ability to share printers, files, and other hardware resources. One printer could be purchased and used by a whole group of users. These early client/server efforts soon led to the need for LAN administration, so more sophisticated software was developed to fill these needs. Early Novell products are a good example of these efforts.

Shortly after these early client/server efforts aimed at sharing hardware, and with the development of faster PC technology and the RISC (reduced instruction set computing) chip for UNIX systems, it became clear that a whole new way of presenting applications was emerging. More expensive computers were purchased for specialized use as file servers, and later as database servers. These servers were shared over the network by a whole range of users with less expensive machines. At the same time, commercially viable database products were providing distributed database tools. INGRESS, for UNIX-based systems, was one of the first to appear (circa 1988).

Recognizing the need to provide presentation tools for the client, software development tools, such as Motif for UNIX machines, began to appear. These early versions of client/server technology that required UNIX systems and RISC technology on the desktop were too expensive for widespread use and did not prove economically viable.

Once the Windows software tools began to appear, and the 386 technology and 486 technology arrived to give some processing power to these PCs, use of client/server technology began to escalate, and small departmental systems began to appear. Developers found that front-end tools like Visual Basic, GUI development tools like PowerBuilder, and Open Data Base Call (ODBC) standards for accessing database servers from Oracle, Informix, Sybase, and Microsoft made distributed database applications much easier.

Meanwhile, these departmental LANs were often purchased without consensus or consideration for what other departments were doing. Nonetheless, the need to interconnect these different LANs to each other, forming enterprise-wide networks, soon emerged. And these enterprise networks began to form even wider-area networks, like the popular Internet. Each of these interconnections was not without a whole host of issues, not the least of which was the agreement on a single protocol to manage and determine the condition of the network and the member LANs and nodes.

Tier Architecture

Desktop presentation applications were divided between thick clients and thin clients. Application architecture was either two-tier or three-tier (see Fig. 2.9). And middleware products began to appear on the scene to help manage the connections between the different parts of the distributed application over the network. Thick clients, those which contained processing rules as well as presentation logic, were usually associ-

Figure 2.9
Two- and three-tier applications.

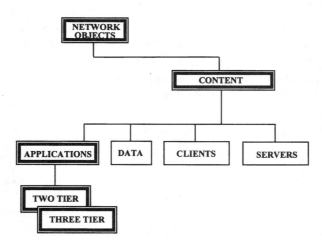

ated with two-tier applications—a Visual Basic front end and an Oracle server, for example.

Thin clients, on the other hand, were associated with three-tier applications, which created a further distribution in the application so that presentation logic was left on the client machines, but other machines held the application logic and still another machine hosted the database. In that way, some scalability was managed by off-loading to the business logic application some of the connection management a database server must provide (see Fig. 2.10).

Application development tools to help build these three-tier applications began to appear. Sybase products like open client and open server provided this functionality, as did CICS for UNIX systems.

At the same time scalability was being addressed, it became apparent that data stores on the mainframe housed important information that the users of these new client/server applications needed to access. This data was not easy to get to in a manner that was transparent to the client applications. Most often the mainframe data resided on one type of network while the client/server applications were connected by another type of network. Tools to address this problem began to appear. The term *gateway* appeared to help application developers get the data that was needed from different networks.

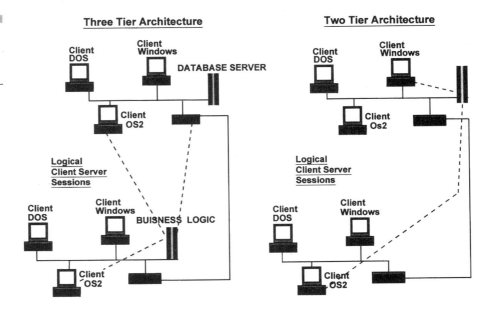

Figure 2.10
Two- and three-tier architecture examples.

Infrastructure

The infrastructure of a computer network describes the way various nodes contact each other and the degree of access each node has to other nodes (see Fig. 3.1). In this chapter the various connection technologies used to provide the different types of network access are discussed, and examples are provided.

Figure 3.1
Infrastructure compo-
nents.

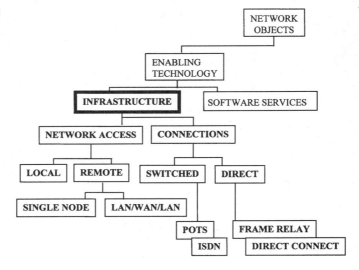

Network Access

Access by nodes to other nodes on a network is described as either local or remote (see Fig. 3.2). *Local access* generally involves nodes located on the same physical network within a close geographical area. Local access nodes are usually supported by token ring or Ethernet LAN technology and do not involve wide area networks or switched connections.

Figure 3.2
Network access archi-
tecture.

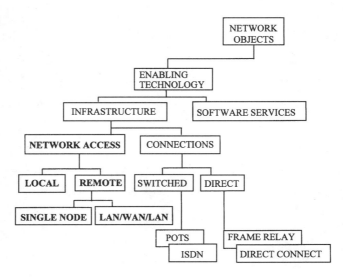

Remote access generally involves nodes that are not locally connected to the LAN on which the server node is located. Remote access is achieved either by remote node—to—LAN access or by LAN-to-LAN access. Remote node—to—LAN access connects one node on the remote LAN to the services of the server LAN. This remote access is gained by either switched or permanent connections. Likewise, LAN-to-LAN access is defined from the LAN on which the remote node is located to the LAN on which the server node exists. In this case, all the nodes of each of the two connected LANS have any-to-any node access. These two different but important configurations are covered in more detail later in the chapter.

Remote Node to LAN

Figure 3.3, "Remote Node—to—LAN Connectivity," shows a PC connected directly to a hosting application LAN over the telephone network. Here two modems are all that is needed to provide the physical connections. Contrast this to Fig. 3.4, "LAN-to-LAN Connectivity," where two LANs are connected together in such a way that any workstation on the LAN can access the application on the hosting application LAN.

This requires a little more thought. But the distinction here is between the remote LAN-to-LAN connection and the remote single

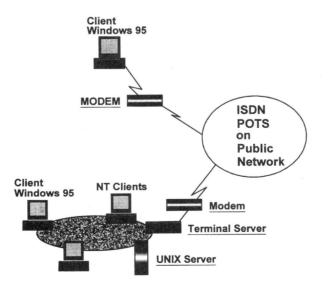

Figure 3.3
Remote node–to–
LAN connectivity.

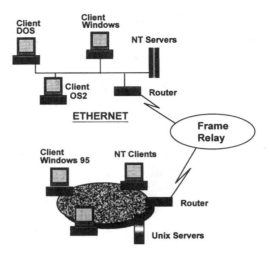

Figure 3.4
LAN-to-LAN connectivity.

user dialing into the hosting application LAN. The primary difference is in the method of connection. Generally a LAN-to-LAN connection will have more bandwidth, be permanent, and require a router-to-router connection for sending packets between the two networks, while a single user can be accommodated with a modem line.

WAN Technologies

Once the application extends its requirement to other local area networks located in different cities, a method has to be found to connect the hosting application network with the nodes, clients, or workstations on the distant LAN. This is the focus of wide area network technology (WANs). Before 1994 there were few alternatives for LAN/WAN/LAN networking, or connecting two LANs together.

Before about 1992, X.25 packet networks were a popular way of providing long-distance data connections, but they were considered inherently slow. In other words, X.25 did not provide sufficient bandwidth, or throughput, to allow multiple clients to access resources over long distances. Although it was OK for one client to access a distant site in this manner, allowing one connection for multiple clients proved too slow.

LAN/WAN/LAN   As discussed, the development of distributed database applications on a single LAN or on a network composed of multiple LANs within the same building creates a number of network and application performance issues. And as the application's requirements extend beyond one network, we have seen how application gateways and routers, also known as gateways, play an enabling role.

To make things more interesting, the application's requirements can extend not only across several networks within the same area, but to users located in different cities and employees traveling on the road. These are, in fact, two separate cases.

LAN to LAN

The WAN-to-LAN connection with SNA access diagram (Fig. 3.5) shows some of the complexity associated with retrieving data from different operating environments over different types of networks. In this example, a LAN is depicted with a router used to connect it to other LANs. A terminal server is used to support users dialing in over the public network. Computers on the LAN host application gateways used to provide access to back-end mainframe systems via the LU6.2 protocol. TCP/IP connections between the various hosts on the LAN are illustrated to show connections to a UNIX database server.

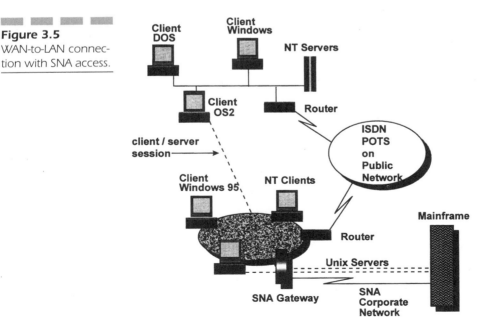

Figure 3.5
WAN-to-LAN connection with SNA access.

Connections

In the past, networks were usually connected together over long distances by point-to-point leased lines from the telephone company. This arrangement proved to be rather expensive, but was suitable for high-value applications. More recently other options have surfaced that have proven less expensive and even faster than leased lines (see Fig. 3.6).

Switched and Direct

The two basic types of communication services available today are switched and direct. *Switched connections* require one of the two endpoints to place a telephone call and the other endpoint to answer. Modems are typically used for the purpose. The circuit is valid until one of the endpoints hangs up the line.

There are a variety of these services. Two of the most popular are plain old telephone service (POTS) and an integrated services digital network (ISDN); the latter requires a special installation.

Direct connections are continuously available end-to-end circuits between two points. The newest example of this is *frame relay*. Frame relay and ISDN are similar offerings; the main distinguishing feature is cost. Frame relay is like the leased line in that a flat fixed fee is charged every month and there is a constant connection between the two LANs

Figure 3.6
Connections and its subgroups.

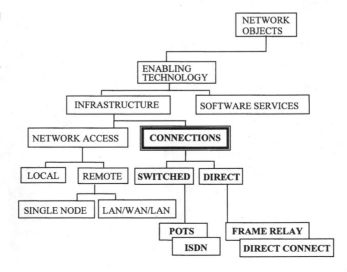

(direct connection). ISDN, a switched service, is charged on a per use basis.

ISDN Services—A Brief Overview

ISDN provides two types of interfaces. One is called *Basic Rate Interface* (BRI), and the other is called *Primary Rate Interface* (PRI). The BRI is the typical implementation for home use, but it is also used in commercial applications as well. The BRI provides for two 64-kbps lines (B channels) and one 16-bit D channel. The B channels are the primary bearer channels and are used to provide the core telephone services, voice and data transmissions. The D channel is used to provide management information and call setup data. BRI implementations are point-to-point circuit connections which consist of seven basic components:

1. *U loop.* This runs between the customer premises and the telephone central office facility.

2. *Terminal adapter (TA).* This is used to provide interoperability with existing equipment standards, such as RS-232 and V.35. These TAs are usually implemented as computer interface cards.

3. *NT-1 (network termination device).* This terminates the U loop at the customer premises. ISDN end-user equipment, such as telephones, faces, or data terminals, can be plugged directly into the NT-1 interface.

4. *S/T bus.* This allows up to eight different devices to share the same ISDN line. The D channel is used to support the management of these devices. No more than one device at a time may access the ISDN line. The D channel is used to send the type of connection request so that only the appropriate device responds (data terminal, fax, voice line, etc.).

5. *TE arbitration.* This is used to ensure that only one device uses the two B channels at a time. Each of the attached ISDN devices listens for requests and responds to appropriately identified incoming transmissions.

6. *Encoding.* Because the data stream scheme used between the telephone company central office (CO) and the NT-1 device is different from the encoding used between the NT-1 and the attached devices, a translation is required. The encoding provides this. The schemes are different because the CO-to-NT-1 device connection is

a single connection from the network, whereas the NT-1-to-attached-device connection was designed to enable channel sharing.

7. *SPIDs* (*service provided IDs*). SPIDs are used by the CO switch to determine the types of services provided to the ISDN device and to identify the devices to the CO switch. A SPID, often a 10-digit number, is encoded and configured on each of the devices on the customer premises as well as at the central office.

Frame Relay

Frame relay is one of the newer networking technologies providing direct connect services. It follows a packet-switching model, but it is implemented in a more efficient manner than the LAPB and X.25 protocols. To make this increased efficiency possible, two assumptions are required.

1. It is assumed that the end devices are intelligent. They have a higher-level protocol that guarantees message integrity.

2. Physical connections have a very low error rate; hence implementation is over fiber optics networks.

Errors are not retransmitted but dropped, and the expectation is that the end devices will detect the missing frame and retransmit the data. The use of TCP/IP over frame relay establishes a robust transport connection over a network, and IP carries data packets. This combination handles retransmission of data errors, a good fit with frame relay.

Data link connections (DLCs) form the basis of frame relay connections. Each DLC has an identifying number called a data link connection identifier (DLCI). The frame relay circuit has a DLCI assigned to both the origination and the termination of the connection. The routine tables in each intervening frame relay switch in the carrier's network route frames to the destination assigned by the DLCI by alternately reading and assigning DLCI values in the control portion of the frames.

ISDN and Frame Relay

ISDN offers available high-throughput bandwidth similar to that provided by frame relay, but as a dial-up or switched service. In other words, the cost is variable and is based on the use of the line, much like your long-distance bill. Therefore, which of these technologies is chosen is a function of cost. If the use of a connection between two sites is high enough for the fixed cost of a frame relay line to be less than the cost of an ISDN line, then frame relay service is chosen. Either way, certain equipment must be purchased. Routers must exist on both ends, and a modemlike device sits in front of each router to connect the lines.

These protocols provide the connectivity between the two sites, but do not provide any ability for applications to communicate. For that, an application protocol like TCP/IP, Novell, SNA, or Netbios is needed. Once this is configured and runs on top of these lower-level connectivity protocols, application functionality is enabled. Until then, it is like having a phone line between two sites, but no telephone at either end to enable conversation. The LAN-to-LAN diagram (Fig. 3.4) shows a fully configured LAN/WAN/LAN connection that is able to support client database applications which can access data on either the local LAN or the remote LAN. Note that TCP/IP is used here to provide the application with access to the underlying data network protocols.

Just as we can have distant LANs with multiple workstations as application users, it is possible to have a single distant user as a client for the business application. These types of clients are almost always enabled through switched service. This can involve single ISDN service, but often it is provided over the existing telephone line.

Plain Old Telephone Service

Modems provide different degrees of throughput, but data transfer rates are measured in thousands of bits per second. So a 28.8-kbps line has a data transfer rate of 28,800 bits per second. This is about the maximum that can be achieved over plain old telephone lines. However, this rate of transfer is often acceptable for a single user subscribing to a database application on a distant LAN.

Perhaps just as difficult to achieve as high bandwidth over copper wire is the client/server feel for a dialed-in user. For this, network implementers rely on Serial Line Internet Protocol (SLIP) or Point-to-Point Protocol (PPP). Both of these provide the basis for application-to-application connections, but do not themselves provide the connections. That requires the use of application-layer protocols. The only such protocol that runs over these types of dialed-in connections is TCP/IP. And this type of configuration is the basis for the public Internet.

Another type of connection, terminal connectivity, can be provided over these dial-up lines. The distinction, though subtle, is most significant. Terminal connections, like those provided by America Online and some of the value-added services, provide programs hosted on a central computer that you dial into as a terminal user. On the other hand, client/server computing over TCP/IP relies on application software on the client computer to talk with application software on the server computer. If this makes no sense now, it is explored more fully as we move along in the book.

Network Services Gateway Connections

Figure 3.7 depicts the connectivity services used by various clients, both local and remote, to access data dispersed on the corporate network on different LANs, running different network protocols (TCP/IP, Novell, SNA), and in different databases or file systems. Key to this implementation is a gateway configured on a LAN which holds a variety of services available to clients seeking data for application services.

As shown in Fig. 3.7, firewall routers isolate the gateway LAN segment. All external connection requests come into devices configured on the outside of the firewall router. This enables the router to filter out all inbound addresses other than those to a particular node, namely the gateway. Once clients are connected to the gateway service, requests going out onto the corporate LAN from the gateway service must originate from the gateway IP address. This limits the exposure to the corporate network and ensures that all external clients have registered with a single point of access.

All data requests coming into the gateway use proxy services to act on their behalf. These proxy services connect the user to the appropriate application on the network and handle any protocol issues. Not shown, but presented in the next chapter, is the security authorization each client connection requires in order to gain access to the proxy agent services.

The different connections, network security services for remote users, routing application requests, and protocol translation so that clients can connect transparently to application services and data are illustrated in Fig. 3.7.

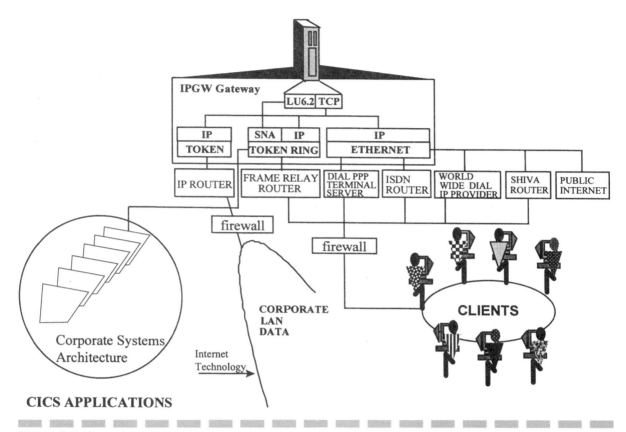

Figure 3.7 Network access architecture.

We have now laid the groundwork for connectivity schemes supporting local clients, remote clients, and clients on remotely attached LANs. The common element for each connection is TCP/IP. These and other topics are covered in the next chapter.

This chapter has looked at the simplest case of the distributed application over a single networked LAN, applications which can span different networks at the same site, and applications which go beyond the same site to provide users in distant cities with access to the business applications. Among these distant users, we have looked at LANs as users and single workstations as users. We have looked at the role of TCP/IP in providing application-to-application connectivity, and we have briefly mentioned terminal connections. Finally, we have examined some of the issues that complicate the single-LAN implementation, multiprotocol networked implementation, and distant user access, whether on a distant LAN or a single workstation.

The remainder of the book discusses many of the networking technologies and topologies introduced here. Particular attention is given to the effects these networking issues have on the client/server application.

Software Services

This chapter discusses those pieces of the enabling technology which enable the client application software to receive services from the network resources. Clients are able to process a variety of transactions to network servers across the network in a secure fashion.

First, the environment in which client/server technology must operate is examined. This includes the variety of computing client environments to be accommodated and the different server environments and database products on the network.

Background

The development of local LAN technology within the organization has been fueled primarily at the local level. This demand-driven process has found a variety of technology solutions for the networking of different resources on local LANs. These solutions have required different proprietary protocol stacks to interconnect the different resources.

There are now at least four major and very different protocol solutions at the local network level: Novel, TCP/IP, Netbios, and SNA mainframe-based protocols.

Novell-based solutions provide users with a whole suite of protocols, LAN management software, and node-to-node connectivity options, like network print drivers and common data sharing on a network drive. However, their proprietary nature, PC-centric architecture, and local LAN management emphasis do not make them very good application client/server enablers. They are very useful, however, for enabling these hardware-sharing features on the LAN.

Netbios is a hardware-centric implementation. Whereas Novell provides a network layer and transport layer, IPX/SPX, Netbios does not. Netbios provides an interface directly to the hardware card on a given LAN. It was developed as a mechanism for a PC on a LAN to talk to other PCs on the same LAN. Named Pipes, the interface used by Netbios for program-to-program communications, gives a program the required session-layer protocols over the local LAN.

Because there is no provision for routing Netbios packets between networks, the usefulness of Netbios is limited to local LAN implementations. However, there are occasions when local LANs running Netbios need to access services on other LANs. Even though many popular Microsoft networking products are based on Netbios, Microsoft provides the user with TCP/IP DLLs for access to the TCP/IP suite of protocols for applications going between LANs. This move in itself has contributed heavily to the development of TCP/IP as a de facto protocol standard.

This leads us to the TCP/IP protocol suite. It is widely used on top of both LAN and WAN connectivity/link-layer protocols, runs over a variety of different link architectures, and is also supported by Novell LAN servers. TCP/IP is one of the key enabling features of the World Wide Web. It is often TCP/IP and some other protocol, Netbios or Novell, that make up the gateways which enable local LANs to access the outside world.

It is not uncommon in the SNA world to find mainframes as member nodes on a LAN technology, particularly token ring. These mainframes, however, are bound together with other nodes on the LAN with IBM's proprietary SNA protocols. It contains all the layers of the OSI model.

Gateways are used between LAN protocols and SNA to get access to data on the mainframe. In fact, SNA mainframe systems are an extremely important part of the nodes on any comprehensive networking plan designed to provide data transparency, as we shall see.

Network Protocols

There are many networking protocol suites in the marketplace today. And, to be sure, there are many more books about each one. But commercial or corporate networks primarily use four different protocol suites: the TCP/IP, Novell, APPN, and Netbios protocols (see Fig. 4.1). And it is not uncommon to have two or three of these running on the same LAN (Windows NT 3.5 and above ships with TCP/IP, Novell's IPX, and Netbios). This chapter reviews these protocols with the idea of giving the reader a basic understanding of how they work and to some extent con-

Figure 4.1
Software services.

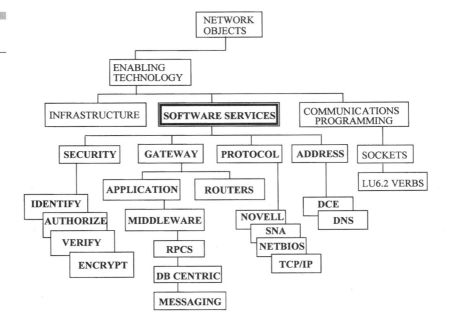

Figure 4-2
Protocol.

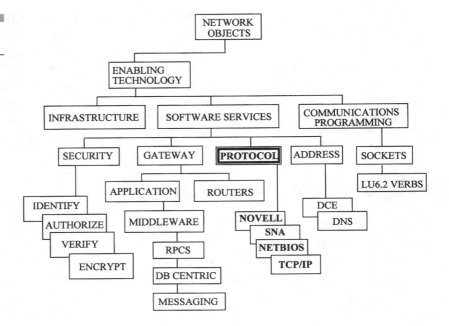

trasting their strengths and weaknesses as network enablers for client/server computing. (See Fig. 4.2.)

TCP/IP

TCP/IP has become so prevalent and important a standard in networking that it is found almost everywhere LAN communication or LAN/WAN/LAN communication is used. Its popularity is due in part to the fact that it is a very robust protocol suite, and in part to the fact that it is absolutely standard among vendors. As well as being the same on Ethernet and token ring LAN connections, it is the same on dial-up async modem connections, ISDN services, and frame relay, and is commonly encapsulated in X.25.

TCP/IP is actually composed of three parts: addressing and routing with IP, guaranteed message delivery using TCP, and application interfaces to the network so that programs can exchange messages (sockets and TLI).

IP Addresses   First, the IP, Internet Protocol, consists of a series of 4-byte addresses separated by dots. These 4 bytes uniquely identify each node in a network and distinguish it from every other node in the world. For example, if the address for a PC is 146.143.240.90, then that 4-byte address is unique throughout all the world. It is, in fact, similar to a telephone number. Other members wishing to communicate with this node simply send all the packets to this IP address.

Besides being a unique addressing scheme for individual nodes, the IP address is also a mechanism for addressing networks within networks. For example, the 146.143.240.90 example consists of two networks, a class B network and a class C network. The class B network is identified by the first 2 bytes of the network IP address. All nodes within that network are further identified by the third byte in the IP address.

For instance, a large corporation may have its entire network designated as 146.143, or the first 2 bytes of the IP address (a class B network). Within this class B network, the corporation may find it convenient to further subdivide its network into class C networks.

In our example (see Fig. 4.3), there is a router whose subnet address is 146.143.240.XX. Within the class C network scheme, each router must be unique up to the first 3 bytes of the Internet address. Since a router is used as the piece of hardware that divides a particular class B network into different class C networks, every node on the different class C networks includes the first 3 bytes of the Internet addressing scheme.

In Fig. 4.3, the node with address 146.143.240.90 is a member of the class C network, or subnet, known as 146.143.240. This subnet, in turn, is a member of a class B network shown as 146.143. Nodes on different class C networks are accessed through routers.

A particular router, besides being a member of the class C network, also connects the network to the other class C networks. The router is used as the portal to the other class C networks defined within the larger class B network. For example, if my address is 146.143.240.15 and I want to send a message to 146.143.240.90, I can do so without the message ever leaving the class C network of which I am a member.

If, on the other hand, I want to send a message to an IP address designated with 146.143.90.12, I am in effect requesting a conversation with another subnet address, controlled by another router on the same class B network, but designating another class C subnet. To get my message there, the packet must travel from my subnet to the 146.143.90.xx router. Here it is forwarded to the designated class C subnet, and then from that router to the target IP address node on that class C network.

To designate a particular node's network membership, a network mask is used. Since there are three primary network types, class A, class B, and class C (class D and class E also exist), there are three separate net-

Figure 4.3
Class B network with
class C subnets.

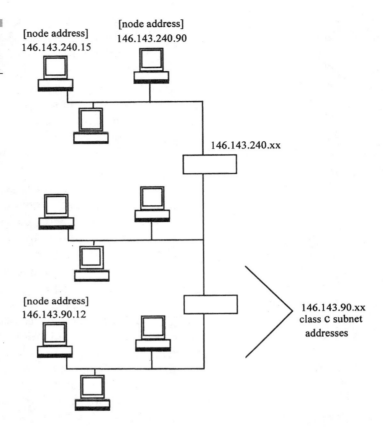

work masks. These are designated as 255.0.0.0 for class A, 255.255.0.0 for class B, and 255.255.255.0 for class C. When used in conjunction with the network IP address, the network mask and the router's address is all the information needed by a PC owner to set up the PC as a member of a worldwide network.

For example, the class C mask, when applied to the IP address in the example, designates that node as a member of the 146.143.240 subnet, and the address for the node on that subnet is 90. With a class B network mask, the network membership would be 146.143 and the node name would be the remainder of the address.

Messages to different nodes are routed over the network through the use of routing tables within the routers. These devices hold the next address for messages coming to them. For example, the IP address for the message is examined by the router, then the next address is determined by looking in the routing table. The next address can be either a network address or the destination node.

Of course, the routing tables, link layer, and physical networking to support this logical IP addressing scheme are more complicated. But the value of IP logical addressing is this very transparency of the addressing scheme to the underlying features of the link and physical layers of the network.

Getting an IP Address. IP addresses for a particular node on a subnet, or router, are a function of the particular router's address. A node is said to be in a particular subnet which is determined by the network class of the subnet. In our examples, nodes on routers that are in class C subnets must have the same 3-byte address as the router that services that subnet. Likewise, routers on class B subnets must have the same address as other routers or nodes on that class B network.

DHCP Addressing. DHCP IP servers are a relative new way of assigning IP addresses to TCP clients that are temporarily connected to a TCP server platform. A pool of IP addresses is made available to a particular server on a LAN, and those addresses are dynamically assigned to a TCP client when a connection is made. The advantages of DHCP addressing are particularly obvious when connections are made temporarily through a dial-up connection via the PPP protocol. In these instances there can be many client machines calling in over phone lines to a server for temporary services.

This is particularly true of World Wide Web and Internet servers. Here the client needs an address on the particular server/router for as long as the connection is set. When the connection is terminated, that address can be used for another client. A much smaller pool of IP resources can be used to communicate with a much larger potential group of clients. The alternative is to assign each potential user a static IP address, whether the client is actually connected to the network or not.

TCP The IP router layer, while greatly simplifying a worldwide communications network for the individual user, does not in fact guarantee the delivery of a message, but simply provides a best effort. In other words, it is possible for a particular message on the IP network to be thrown away if traffic exceeds capacity. In fact, all messages exceeding capacity at a given point of the network could simply be tossed. The network IP layer does not ensure delivery, it only routes what it can.

Should a packet get discarded, that must be detected by the TCP layer at the individual workstations that are in conversation with each other. It is at the TCP layer, layer 4, that error recovery and retransmission is achieved, unlike the situation with the SNA SDLC protocol, where delivery is assured at the link layer. TCP then exists between the endpoints of a conversation between the workstations and is not found anywhere else in the network, like the routers or bridges. These components are built for network connectivity and network routing, not for delivery. As such, the intervening components between two end nodes that are talking are totally transparent to the TCP workstation layer.

As discussed earlier, associated with each layer of a network protocol is a packet layer. Each packet is included totally within the layer below it. As such, all IP packets contain complete TCP packets, and any link-layer packets, like Ethernet, token ring, or frame relay, contain the IP packets. As this extended packet travels up the protocol stack to the layer above, each encasing is removed. In that way, the TCP layer has its own set of protocols to ensure message delivery and the IP layer can remain oblivious to message delivery.

Sockets   Just as TCP ensures message delivery and the IP layer is used for packet routing, the *socket* protocol is used to give programs on the desktop access to the particular network. It is at this layer that client/server architecture begins to have some meaning and the application begins to take on a business value. Sockets represent a set of well-architected interfaces that allow messages to go from an application program onto the network and to be retrieved by an application program at the other end.

Hence, clients use socket calls to send requests to a server and receive responses from a server. And servers use socket calls to listen for messages from clients, accept the connections from the clients, read the messages, and send back responses. This architecture provides a consistent interface to TCP via the socket calls used to distinguish different sessions, and the IP layer can remain oblivious to sessions.

Integrating TCP/IP on the LAN with Network Operating Systems

Among existing protocols, the most prevalent on corporate LANs are Novell and Netbios (see Fig. 4.2). To enable multiple protocols on a LAN, or specifically to exist on the workstation or server, two types of device drivers are prevalent. These are known as Network Device Interface specification (NDIs) and Open Data-Link Interface (ODI).

NDIS drivers are of two types, protocol drivers and media access control (MAC) drivers. The MAC driver is at the bottom of the protocol stack and is the driver that interfaces directly with the hardware (adapter driver). The MAC driver transmits and receives packets. The upper drivers (protocol drivers) implement various higher-level communications services by handling the different network data formats (IP and IPX, for example). A vector layer within NDIS sits on the adapter driver and allows two different protocol stacks to coexist on the same adapter card (see Fig. 4.4). Therefore, Novell protocol stacks and TCP/IP stacks can exist on a single adapter driver or on a single network interface card.

NDIS is largely concerned with defining functions that determine how the MAC driver communicates with the protocols found on the upper level.

Implemented to perform the same function, ODI from Novell defines a logical link control that accepts packets from the media driver. These two link-layer drivers enable different protocol stacks to sit above them and use the same card or have the same stack use different cards.

Multiple link interface drivers (MLIDs) are written for each type of network connectivity, such as Ethernet boards, token ring boards, and FDDI boards. A link support layer (LSL) sits on the MLID and receives communications from it. These are then passed to the appropriate network driver through a series of interfaces.

Whichever method of support is used on the workstation, the same method must be used on all of them. NDIS drivers talk to NDIS drivers and cannot talk to ODI drivers. Assuming an appropriate choice, this section addresses the integration of TCP/IP onto the LAN with existing Novell protocols.

This primarily involves integrating various computing services between TCP servers and Netware servers. These include

1. Terminal emulation

2. Basic file transfer

3. Advanced file transfer

4. Printing services

Figure 4.4
Relationship of NDIS
to the OSI stack.

5. Electronic mail

6. Client/server facilities

7. Database support

There are three ways to support this. More than one of these is often required to support the array of business services listed above. But each method nonetheless has its own costs and benefits. All the approaches involve maintaining both the Netware IPX/SPX protocol stack and the TCP/IP protocol stack. The three methods are:

1. Teach UNIX systems to speak Netware.

2. Teach Netware systems to support UNIX.

3. Provide a gateway or translator between the two.

Each of these integration strategies presupposes an array of different networking products to support the various services listed above.

UNIX Supporting NETWARE   This approach entails the use of an IPX/SPX protocol suite and various Novell products on the UNIX platform. It has the advantage of requiring no changes to the existing NOS/DOS platforms. It is the strategy behind the "netware for UNIX" products.

Netware for UNIX is shipped with NVT, which allows terminal emulation to the UNIX host through the IPX/SPX protocol. Once logged into the specific UNIX platform hosting the NVT program, users may Telnet or RLOGIN over the existing TCP/IP network.

The net effect of this approach is to maintain two separate networks, each running a different protocol, and use the Netware for UNIX product to support file sharing and terminal access between them. It further implies the use of a single UNIX server to host the network files, with that UNIX platform designated as a Novell server.

Additionally, that UNIX platform is used like a terminal server in that clients must login to it using IPX/SPX sessions before Telnet or RLOGIN can be used to go to other TCP/IP UNIX hosts.

NETWARE Speaking UNIX   More specifically, this entails the installation of TCP/IP protocol stacks on the DOS/NOS Novell platforms to enable facilities like Telnet, RLOGIN, NFS, FTP, print sharing between UNIX and NOVELL platforms, SNMP-supported e-mail, and client application software typically using the socket protocol. This includes a variety of SQL database products.

This networking strategy is behind all the Netware NFS products and FLEXip products, the stand-alone PC packages that add TCP/IP, and the NFS, TELNET, and socket API programmable interfaces for client/server computing which use TCP.

With NDIS architecture, it is quite common to find both the TCP/IP protocol and the Netware native IPX protocol coresident on the PC.

The net effect of this approach is to add the TCP/IP protocol suite onto the Netware LAN. This is considerably different from the first approach in that a common protocol is used over the physical Ethernet LAN; this provides an open architecture which allows any platform to send and receive information from any other platform. It does not limit file services to one UNIX platform, nor does it require the use of a specific UNIX server as a terminal server to the rest of the network.

Using a GATEWAY (TCP/IP to SPX/IPX)   Using this approach, Novell NOS/DOS clients communicate with the gateway through an IPX session, which then gets translated to a TCP/IP session to the UNIX host. Telnet sessions are then open for terminal emulation, file transfer, and file sharing. Client/server computing is not so straightforward however.

Gateways between Novell and TCP/IP are also necessary for supporting e-mail applications and print sharing.

Support for Client/Server Computing.   The client's choice of SQL databases is limited when the database must fit into a Netware IPX/SPX environment. And if the database runs in a UNIX environment, DOS/client access over Novell will be through terminal login sessions.

Client applications running over Novell to connect to the SQL UNIX server are few and generally require the existence of a protocol converter between the front-end Novell client and the back-end TCP/IP-based UNIX SQL database.

It is not likely that this situation will change in the near term, since there is no Novell equivalent to a UNIX TCP/IP Domain Name Service (DNS), a product which allows clients to connect to servers located at various nodes on the network.

Support Options for E-mail and Print Sharing.   Without the TCP/IP protocol over both physical segments, both e-mail support between different platforms and print sharing between Novell clients on a UNIX platform will require the use of gateways.

Conclusions   Any solution which does not offer a common protocol suite like TCP/IP both over the physical LAN segments and on each of the LAN nodes limits future computing options and offers little more flexibility than exists today.

Therefore, providing the client with a Netware for UNIX product offers very little more than the existing network configuration offers.

NFS/file sharing would be supported from the UNIX server only, and would not be available from other UNIX platforms on the network except through a multistep process that may be too complicated for the average user to perform.

No client/server capability is inherent in this approach. Access to UNIX SQL databases is limited to terminal logins to the server over IPX/SPX sessions. And the approach inherently creates a single point of failure on the LAN for access to the UNIX machines.

Even though there may be additional cost associated with the development of both TCP/IP and Novell protocol stacks on the PC platforms, the functionality achieved will create the objective: open networking.

UNIX/Novell integration with Netware running on UNIX platforms is an investment in a limiting architecture which does not provide much flexibility and reduces the capability of UNIX machines. It offers no longer-term improvement in computing capability, with upgradable paths difficult to achieve. Nor will it give straightforward solutions for e-mail and client/server computing.

IBM's APPN Alternative for SNA Networks

Although IBM has not been very successful in porting APPN technology to the desktop, most SNA networks are now APPN (advanced peer-to-peer network) networks.

The APPN technology from IBM not only provides a routing protocol including intermediate routing, topology, and route selection, but also provides configuration services, session services, and management services. There is a lot to be said about this network routing service. After a little background, I'd like to comment on the way it can simplify the process of target resource identification for a requester, or, put another way, facilitate client/server computing.

Overview   SNA APPN is IBMs networking protocol (OSI layer 3). It operates at the same level as X.25 and IP. At the networking layer, it can act as a LAN/WAN protocol router. Unlike other routing protocols, APPN defines a hierarchy of participating peers, with some apparently being more equal than others. Three different node functions are defined: network node (NN), end node (EN), and low-entry networking (LEN), another end node. Each of these nodes supports a 2.1 physical unit, and hence supports application program-to-program connectivity (APPC) through LU6.2 verb calls. This means, of course, that application-layer programs use the LU6.2 verbs to provide APPC over the APPN network nodes. The degree to which these nodes participate in the network is a function of the node type (NN, EN, or LEN).

APPN, now available on OS/2, and hence a networking option for PC LANs, is typically set up with at least one NN node. This node provides all the routing and session services for other attached ENs, and the EN need not know anything else about other network resources on the LAN to receive APPC service. Each of the EN platforms is configured to the NN via a control point (CP) session (LU6.2), and the NN provides a directory service of all the other nodes on the network and the resources they contain (LUs).

Among other things, the NN does the routing to the requested network resource and performs the session connections between the requesting node (LU) application and the target LU or application program. Because these two types of nodes (NN and EN) provide these services as a function of APPN, dynamic configuration and routing is automatic. When an EN platform enters service or exits service, the CP-to-CP sessions established between the NN and the EN exchange network resource information.

In contrast, the low-entry networking node is a poorer cousin of these dynamic pairs. Although LEN nodes provide application-to-application connectivity with other networking nodes, they must be completely configured with the address of the network node and LU they want to contact, and they are not configured dynamically when they come into or go out of service.

As a LAN/WAN routing protocol, each connected LAN is serviced through the NN. Because IBM has made APPN technology available, many vendors offer NN-capable services. System Strategies, makers of EZBRIDGE, Novell, and Apple, through Appletalk, plan to provide APPN connectivity. Therefore, any or all of these different LAN protocols could be serviced by an existing SNA backbone WAN to enable not only participation in the SNA network, but data sharing among different LANs of the same type connected to the WAN using APPC protocol.

Like a Domain Name Server But Better? The NN provides much the same services to applications running on the network as the Domain Name Server (DNS) provides to TCP/IP hosted client/server computing. For example, with sockets TCP/IP or Remote Procedure Calls (RPCs), the requesting client calls the DNS to get the address of the service being provided. Then, using a port number (like a logical unit), it accesses the service on a given host. In this sense APPN provides both routing and transport-layer services (IP and TCP) to the application in the APPC/LAN environment. In a programming environment, use of LU6.2 APPC or CPI-C interfaces with APPN makes network resource location completely transparent to the communications programmer.

Unlike the case in the socket TCP/IP environment or the RPC code, not only are explicit calls required in order to register the server with the DNS, but the client must call the DNS explicitly to find the address of the server being connected to. In contrast to sockets TCP/IP, the APPN/APPC programmer must know the name of the LU representing the target application and know the name of the target application itself, as one LU can represent many target applications.

Unlike RPCs, the APPN/APPC environment still provides no XDR translator service. And APPC verbs provide no inherent discipline on the data being passed (i.e., data is a string, not arguments to a function, as RPCs provide). However, in contrast to socket programming, a clear advantage of APPN/APPC is the location transparency of the target resource being requested.

Netbios

Netbios is not a protocol, it is a software interface between a program and the actual hardware interface card. Netbios provides four types of service: name, session, datagram, and general commands.

Names identify Netbios resources. Unique names are used to identify individual resources. Netbios is designed to work with LAN segments. Because Netbios is not a protocol but an interface, it is not routable across different LAN segments, as TCP/IP is, for example. There are, however, implementations of Netbios which use TCP/IP as the transport/network interfaces. Because Netbios has been around so long and is functional on individual LAN segments, it is in common use. Microsoft Windows for Workgroups uses an implementation of Netbios. Beginning with Windows NT 3.5, however, NWLINK replaces Netbios as the Windows standard. NWLINK is Internetwork Packet Exchange (IPX) for Netware. Besides including these protocols, Windows NT 3.5 also provides TCP/IP as standard on the network.

Netbios was designed for use by groups of PCs sharing a broadcast medium. Both connection (session) and connectionless (datagram) services are provided, and broadcast and multicast are supported. Participants are identified by name. Assignment of names is distributed and highly dynamic.

Netbios applications employ Netbios mechanisms to locate resources, establish connections, send and receive data with an application peer, and terminate connections. For purposes of discussion, these mechanisms will collectively be called the Netbios service.

This service can be implemented in many different ways. One of the first implementations was for personal computers running the PC-DOS and MS-DOS operating systems. It is possible to implement Netbios within other operating systems, or as processes which are, themselves, simply application programs as far as the host operating system is concerned.

Interface to Application Programs   Netbios on personal computers includes both a set of services and an exact program interface to those services. On other computer systems, Netbios may present the Netbios services to programs using other interfaces. Except on personal computers, no clear standard for a Netbios software interface has emerged.

Name Service   Netbios resources are referenced by name. Lower-level address information is not available to Netbios applications. An application, representing a resource, registers one or more names that it wishes to use.

The name space is flat and uses 16 alphanumeric characters. Names may not start with an asterisk (`*`).

Registration is a bid for use of a name. The bid may be for exclusive (unique) or shared (group) ownership. Each application contends with the other applications in real time. Implicit permission is granted to a station when it receives no objections. That is, a bid is made and the application waits for a period of time. If no objections are received, the station assumes that it has permission.

A unique name should be held by only one station at a time. However, duplicates ("name conflicts") may arise as a result of errors. All instances of a group name are equivalent.

An application referencing a name generally does not know (or care) whether the name is registered as a unique or a group name.

An explicit name deletion function is specified, so that applications may remove a name. Implicit name deletion occurs when a station ceases operation. In the case of personal computers, implicit name deletion is a frequent occurrence.

Name Service Primitives.   There are three name service primitives:

1. *Add Name.* The requesting application wants exclusive use of the name.
2. *Add Group Name.* The requesting application is willing to share use of the name with other applications.
3. *Delete Name.* The application no longer requires use of the name. It is important to note that Netbios is typically used among independently operated personal computers. A common way to stop using a PC is to turn it off; in this case, the graceful giveback mechanism provided by the Delete Name function is not used. Because this behavior occurs frequently, the network service must support it.

Session Service   A session is a reliable message exchange, conducted between a pair of Netbios applications. Sessions are full-duplex, sequenced, and reliable. Data is organized into messages. Each message may range in size from 0 to 131,071 bytes. No expedited or urgent data capabilities are present.

Multiple sessions may exist between any pair of calling and called names, and the parties to a connection have access to the calling and called names.

The Netbios specification does not define how a connection request to a shared (group) name resolves into a session. The usual assumption is that a session may be established with any one owner of the called group name.

An important service provided to Netbios applications is the detection of session failure. The loss of a session is reported to an application via all of the outstanding service requests for that session. For example, if the application has a Netbios receive primitive pending and the session terminates, the pending receive will abort with a termination indication.

Session Service Primitives.   There are six session service primitives:

1. *Call.* This initiates a session with a process that is listening under the specified name. The calling entity must indicate both a calling name (properly registered to the caller) and a called name.

2. *Listen.* This accepts a session from a caller. The listen primitive may be constrained to accept an incoming call from a named caller. Alternatively, a call may be accepted from any caller.

3. *Hang Up.* This gracefully terminates a session. All pending data is transferred before the session is terminated.

4. *Send.* This transmits one message. A time-out can occur. A time-out of any session send forces the nongraceful termination of the session.

A Chain Send primitive is required by the PC Netbios software interface to allow a single message to be gathered from pieces in various buffers. Chain Send is an interface detail and does not affect the protocol.

5. *Receive.* This receives data. A time-out can occur. A time-out on a session receive terminates only the receive, not the session, although the data is lost.

The receive primitive may be implemented with variants, such as Receive Any, which is required by the PC Netbios software interface. Receive Any is an interface detail and does not affect the protocol.

6. *Session Status.* This obtains information about all of the requestor's sessions, under the specified name. No network activity is involved.

Datagram Service   The datagram service is an unreliable, nonsequenced, connectionless service. Datagrams are sent under cover of a name properly registered to the sender.

Datagrams may be sent to a specific name or may be explicitly broadcast. Datagrams sent to an exclusive name are received, if at all, by the holder of that name. Datagrams sent to a group name are multicast to all holders of that name. The sending application program cannot distinguish between group and unique names and thus must act as if all nonbroadcast datagrams are multicast.

As with the session service, the receiver of the datagram is told the sending and receiving names.

Datagram Service Primitives.   There are four datagram service primitives:

1. *Send Datagram.* This sends an unreliable datagram to an application that is associated with the specified name. The name may be unique or group; the sender is not aware of the difference. If the name belongs to a group, then each member is to receive the datagram.

2. *Send Broadcast Datagram.* This sends an unreliable datagram to any application with a Receive Broadcast Datagram posted.

3. *Receive Datagram.* This receives a datagram sent by a specified originating name to the specified name. If the originating name is an asterisk, then the datagram may have been originated under any name.

Note: An arriving datagram will be delivered to all pending Receive Datagrams that have source and destination specifications matching those of the datagram. In other words, if a program (or group of programs) issues a series of identical Receive Datagrams, one datagram will cause the entire series to complete.

4. *Receive Broadcast Datagram.* This receives a datagram sent as a broadcast. If there are multiple pending Receive Broadcast Datagram operations pending, all will be satisfied by the same received datagram.

Miscellaneous Functions   The following functions are present to control the operation of the hardware interface to the network. These functions are generally implementation-dependent.

1. *Reset.* This function initializes the local network adapter.
2. *Cancel.* This function aborts a pending Netbios request. The successful Cancel of a Send (or Chain Send) operation will terminate the associated session.
3. *Adapter Status.* This function obtains information about the local network adapter or a remote adapter.
4. *Unlink.* This function is used with Remote Program Load (RPL). Unlink redirects the PC boot disk device back to the local disk.
5. *Remote Program Load.* Remote Program Load is not a Netbios function. It is a Netbios application defined by IBM in its Netbios specification.

Gateway

The term *gateway* can refer to two different network functions (see Fig. 4.5). Gateway is often used to mean router, which is a piece of equipment that operates at layer 3 in the OSI reference model.

Routers

A router gateway usually connects a local LAN with a larger network, like a corporate internet. More often than not, the router can be used to

Software Services

Figure 4.5
Gateway and its sub-groups.

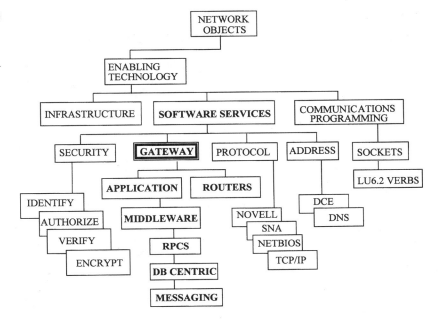

translate between different physical- and link-layer protocols. For example, IP protocols run at layer 3, the routing layer. However, IP may also run on top of Ethernet or token ring link layers, so a router can be used as a gateway between different link- and physical-layer connections. Software in the router takes Ethernet link packets and sends them up to the IP routing layer. The IP routing layer then sends them back down to the token ring, where they are on their way (see Fig. 4.6).

Other gateways are used to encapsulate different protocols. For example, TCP/IP packets can get encapsulated as X.25 packets to get from one LAN in one city across the WAN to a LAN in another city (see Fig. 4.7). This is an older technology; such LAN/WAN/LAN requirements are now being handled via frame relay (level 2) connections and ISDN (point-to-point) switched connections. I refer to these as examples; they will be discussed in more detail later.

An application gateway, on the other hand, encompasses all seven layers of the OSI model, and is used to translate very different network architectures so that application-layer programs can talk to one another. One of the most common of these is used to translate TCP/IP networks to SNA networks. This is the function of many of the so-called SQL gateways that go between Windows and mainframe applications. Products like MDI gateways are specific to TCP/IP-to-SNA network protocol

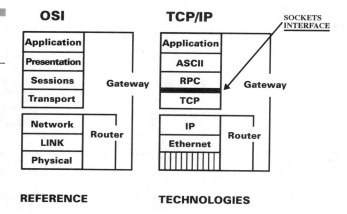

Figure 4.6
Gateway protocol
stacks.

Figure 4.7
Data protocol
formats.

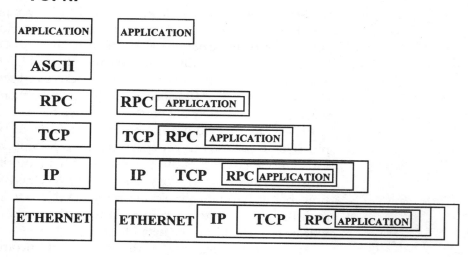

translation and also include translation of different SQL data query languages.

Oracle provides a variety of application gateways that create transparency between different LAN networking technologies. These include TCP/IP to Netbios. Additionally, Novell provides translation to its

IPX/SPX protocol to allow Novell users to participate in TCP/IP networks. Installing these gateways and getting them to work properly often requires configuration and some knowledge of network protocols to install them.

Application

There are two networking approaches that support cooperative processing between any two platforms: homogeneous (one protocol stack) and gateway networking.

Homogeneous Networking vs. Gateway Connectivity

In a homogeneous network, each computer belongs to the same network and is considered an addressable node by any other node in the network. This is the case when one protocol stack is used to connect the various nodes. A homogeneous network is defined by one protocol stack.

When feasible, implementing client/server over one network is the best solution. It creates a straightforward solution for resource sharing among the host nodes. To achieve maximum benefit over a homogeneous network, consistency among platform operating systems must be considered.

Failing a one-protocol solution, the alternative for providing resource sharing is the use of gateway products which translate between the different protocol stacks on two separate networks. This architecture provides resource sharing, but at the extra cost of integration, such as CPU resources to do the protocol conversion, and more software development time.

The solution of integration between different platforms leaves the environment on each platform in place, and uses a gateway to achieve the application-to-application connections. This gateway uses two seven-layer protocol stacks to translate between the two different networks to achieve the application-to-application connections.

As such, gateways provide physical-, link-, network-, and transport-layer translation. Most stacks support a variety of link-layer protocols, including SNA SDLC, token ring (802.3), and Ethernet (802.4). Others support different routing-layer semantics between SNA and TCP or TCP and Novell. Depending on the current configuration of the network and the objectives of the connectivity, one of these options will better serve the business goals.

The gateway provides several key application services. The gateway access architecture diagram (see Fig. 4.8) depicts these and their relative position within the network and on the network stacks. This figure shows a client hosting an application running on the TCP/IP stack and connecting to the gateway server over a WAN protocol.

Certain application services have been identified as appropriate for the gateway to perform. Besides the security functions described previously, these include logging requests with date and time, store and forward, communication acknowledgments, messaging, and recovery. These are developed in Chap. 5.

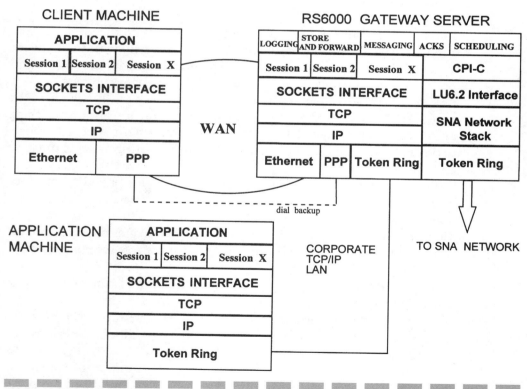

Figure 4.8 Gateway access architecture.

Application Network Management

In this discussion, network management is differentiated from application network management. In the former, the nodes on the network are continuously monitored. This is usually done by the network management group. In an application monitor, the software services are monitored for problems. Any uncertainties or failures are reported to the monitor interactively, and the failure of a service is also reported.

Network management is implemented as a service on top of the TCP/IP layers. The most sensitive is the gateway platform. Here APIs are used to send messages to a graphics monitor which shows the various transactions occurring in the system, the origin of those transactions, and their current state.

The last transaction of the same type from the same source is left on the monitor as a way of checking current status. Pings to servers are periodically issued to determine the status of different network services. Failures are reported from the gateway to the applications monitor. The monitoring efforts then can proactively discover problems with applications before the user actually notices them, and corrective action can be taken. That is the goal; however, it is not always realized.

Application Services Provided by the Gateway

This section briefly discusses four additional software infrastructure services provided on the gateway, where the gateway becomes the point of access for external users, and in some instances for internal users as well.

External Users of Gateway Services　For security purposes (discussed in detail in Chap. 7), all external users enter the corporate network through a single access point, and execute all services on the corporate network via proxy agents on the gateway.

Logging Functions　The gateway provides a single point of application logging for all requests for proxy services. Transaction data as received from the client and as returned to the client are logged. Along with transaction data, the originating address of the request is recorded, and each transaction request and response is time-stamped. Any errors encountered by any of the proxy services on the gateway are also logged here as well as being sent to the application monitor.

Store and Forward There are two popular meanings for *store and forward*. One refers to the asynchronous protocol whereby messages are passed along from one platform to the next in a series of chains until they reach their final destination. At each node on the network chain through which the messages pass, they are stored or buffered. The messages are then re-sent to the next node, where the same process takes place.

In the application context, store and forward describes a process whereby an intervening service will hold messages for a particular client even though the application service may not be readily available. For example, the gateway software holds trade transactions for delivery at a later time once the requested service has resumed. These transactions are usually held in a persistent storage queue (file) until the target service comes back on-line. Once the service is on-line, the transactions are forwarded to the application. IBM's MQ series product is based on this technology, and it forms the basis for continuous processing.

The alternative to store and forward is to return a service unavailable error to the client program.

Although the MQ series is built on an asynchronous store-and-forward technology, synchronous store-and-forward solutions are also common. In these implementations, the client forwards the request to a proxy gateway service. This service then forwards the request to the destination service. Once the request is received by the destination service, the proxy service on the gateway returns a response to the client.

Should the proxy service be unable to deliver the request on behalf of the client, the request can be held and forwarded later, with a different response code issued to the client, or a retry response can be issued. Socket-based TCP/IP transport services are often implemented as synchronous services.

Messaging As will be touched on in the discussion of middleware, messaging is but one class of products of this type.

Messaging refers to a class of middleware, whether implemented via commercial packages or built with native socket and LU6.2 APIs, which provides standard protocol delivery. This is in contrast to systems which provide database-centric SQL network implementations built on vendor proprietary transport systems like Oracle or Sybase. In the case of Sybase, a set of tools known as Open Server is provided to give the developer a window into the SQL queries, read them, and provide additional services for the connection service.

Although these proprietary connections are often referred to as messages, they are not messages, in that they are intended to be processed by another service which also understands proprietary protocols, such as a SQL server. These types of systems are inherently two-tier. Clients intend to deliver a proprietary request for service to another proprietary service. The gateway does *not* support any application services for two-tier application solutions.

What is provided is an API available to the client to send messages to and receive them from a particular gateway service. These APIs allow programs to send and receive asynchronously. The APIs consist of calls which have corresponding verbs on the gateway. These calls also include the security APIs needed to do service authorization and then message verification. The use of native socket APIs and their ownership by the gateway simplify the communications process to the application. The use of socket APIs reduces the number of vendor proprietary protocols needed on a given client machine.

Middleware

On top of this gateway stack, and utilizing the provided interfaces to the transport layer, a middleware product may be employed to simplify connectivity interfaces (see Fig. 5.1). *The important and limiting requirement is that every platform must employ the middleware and the middleware, as an application, must run on each of the platforms.*

Important, but often obscured, is the fact that "the middleware is not the gateway." The gateway is the two network stacks; the middleware sits on top of those two stacks on the gateway and on each node which uses the gateway.

Distributed client/server database transactions are of two types:

Figure 5.1
Middleware and its
subgroups.

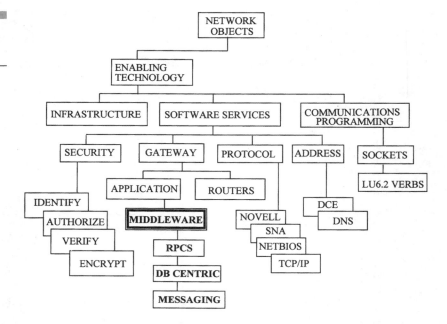

1. Decision support systems where data is supplied to users in distributed locations from some central source

2. Distributed transaction applications where data is supplied to the central source from various distributed points

   Within these two types of client/server applications, there are three typical implementations of middleware support products:

1. Database-centric applications using specific products like Oracle client/server products and Visual Basic products.

2. Synchronous support using Remote Procedure Calls (RPCs) provided by Distributed Computing Environment (DCE) architecture, where called routines are stored in a server library and made available to RPC clients residing on various nodes on the customer-defined network

3. Finally, asynchronous access supported by the MQ series product, the CICS6000 product, and other "specified" architectures

   Depending on the product, middleware provides several functions:

   1. *Transaction monitor.* This ensures that the application on the client machine is informed about the disposition of requested database service

on the server machine (i.e., did the update, delete, or add take place as expected; if not, what happened).

2. *Connection manager.* Clients requesting data services from a server must connect to that server. As the number of connections grows, this can produce extra overhead for the database server, which most are ill-equipped to manage. A connection manager handles those requests and generally improves the scalability and response time for large numbers of clients seeking simultaneous access.

3. *Network latency reduction.* The time it takes an application to send a request for database services and get a response from the service is a function of, among other things, the number of nodes the request must transverse to get to the server node (intermediate routers, etc.). This wait time for the application is most apparent in synchronous applications. Those are defined as applications which *wait* for the response before returning to the user for more work to be performed.

Middleware products provide an intermediate method of storage for the client application on the client platform (either a queue or a file). These products store data requests on the client machine; a background process then reads that intermediate storage and sends the request to the database server. Likewise, server nodes equipped with a comparable product read the network message and put it into a queue to be read by the server application.

This method allows the client application to deposit the data request into the queue and then go do other things. It intermittently checks the queue in a polling environment for responses from the server or, in the case of an interrupt-driven response, receives messages from the queue when data has arrived from the server. Network latency doesn't get reduced, but from the point of view of the application, it has been all but eliminated.

4. *Network monitor.* A fourth purpose of some middleware products is to provide proactive network monitoring for application servers. It is questionable whether these products should be considered middleware, as this service is often provided by the database server.

As previously discussed, three types of middleware products are gaining particular dominance in the market place. To recapitulate, these are:

1. Database-centric products which provide middleware services within the context of the database product suite, such as Oracle, Sybase, or Informix.

2. Synchronous models, which imply a complete network architecture like DCE and the associated RPCs as well as products built on top of them like CICS6000 and Encina.

3. Asynchronous methods, often called messaging. These incorporate local queues to store data to be transported around the network. These include IBM's MQ series and other specified products. Products of this type are usually thought of as productivity tools. They are not "solutions," but rather facilitate design and programming to ensure transaction monitoring. Some also provide tools for formatting transactions for applications, but these often imply standards which must be adopted within the application design.

Most large corporations very likely have all three implemented in different network client/server applications.

There are basic challenges for middleware solutions and vendors. To be of value, these products must run on different platforms, under different operating systems, and over different communication protocols (see Fig. 5.2).

For companies specializing in these products, the cost of maintaining such an offering is often greater than the revenue realized from the sale. Customers find these products require specialized and expensive labor to implement and are often costly to maintain. Also, given the rapidly changing market conditions and highly competitive nature of the client/server distributed world, the life-cycle value of middleware purchases should be considered carefully.

Given this qualification, the products addressed here are among the three most popular solutions: the Distributed Computing Environment (DCE), the Sybase Open Server and Open Client architecture, and finally the MQ series.

DCE (RPCs)

Remember reading about DCE from the Open Systems Foundation several years ago? It promised a sort of network application nirvana where any-to-any access to a node and the resources it owned would be available to any other user, and client/server computing would be implemented by Remote Procedure Calls that took the "communications" out of communications programming. User IDs for the entire network would be administered at a single point, and, best of all, the mainframe

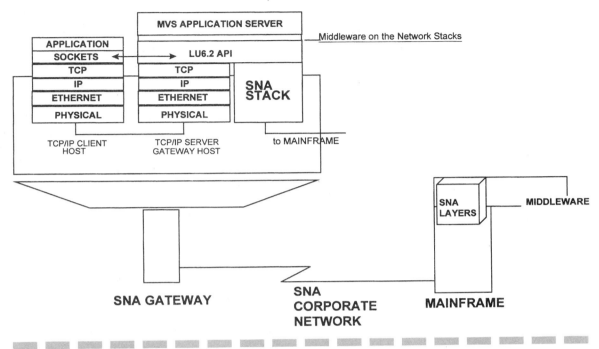

Figure 5.2 Components of middleware architecture.

would be like any node on the network. In essence, Windows, UNIX, MVS, and OS/2 would live and work together in harmony.

Some progress has been made since the days of vaporware. There is a version of DCE available which runs over IBM's NETANY API and TCP/IP that fulfills some, if not all, of these promises previously mentioned.

There are two major benefits provided by DCE. The first is network/LAN administration, including security; the other is client/server software development.

Network/LAN Administration

For DCE to be really useful, it requires a buy-in from the entire organization. That's because DCE is built to administer multiple LAN sites through the use of *cells,* with a cell being defined as any group of users who have more or less the same business mission (i.e., share the same data resources). DCE is implemented in three basic parts, each of which is designed to make LAN administration and LAN security a more manageable process. These include DCE Security Services, Distributed File Services, and DCE Directory Services. Each of these services is implemented within a given cell and set up so that intercell sharing is possible, if not very efficient.

DCE Security Services add more value than other LAN administration services, as they allow separate security definitions for logins, clients, services, and database resources.

DCE Distributed File Services provide much the same access as NIS (previously yellow pages), with the ability to mount files on servers as they become available to the network (of course, plenty of products do that).

DCE Directory Services (DDS) perform the same function as Domain Name Services (DNS) in that they provide a network addressing scheme whereby clients who wish to connect with different servers on the network can look up the servers' location and automatically connect to the service needed. By the way, DCE works with either DNS or DDS, but not both. If you have need of a central repository for network services, you probably have DNS installed.

Different parts of these DCE services are more or less available on different platforms. It's a good idea to check. For example, DCE Distributed File Services are not available on the OS/2 platform, but the Security and Directory Services are. The mainframe DCE piece may not be as useful as it is costly, not to mention getting agreement to install it. The DCE administration does, however, initiate a path to network application resource sharing.

The second part of DCE involves software development for client/server applications, a phrase as tired as the benefits are illusive. Perhaps RPC/DCE, much like Sun RPC, which has been around for a long time, can help bring client/server computing benefits home. This, I think, is optimistic, since RPC implementation is a solution that is more complicated than the problem it solves. And up to now RPCs have not caught on as a replacement for socket or TLI programming. However, a discussion of the client/server development process may help point out the benefits of using RPCs.

Client/Server Software Development

Network servers provide some service to any number of clients on a network. In writing these servers and the clients that use them, there are four primary decisions to be made. First, what service does the server provide to the client? Second, where is the server located? Third, how do I get to it? And fourth, what data do I send it and what do I get back (including error codes)?

Of course, RPCs won't help in determining what the service is going to do, but they can help in implementing the other three components: finding the service from the client, getting to it, and defining the data interfaces to the service.

Typically, using the TCP/IP protocol, servers execute on a particular platform which has an IP address, and on that platform the servers listen on a port number. For the client to connect, it must know the IP address of the host the server is on, and it must know the port number where the server is listening. Knowing that, the client requests the service through socket calls or TLI interface calls. Once the client is connected to the server, the server typically starts the service the client has requested [usually a fork()] and connects the new process to the client.

Data is then exchanged between the client and the server through some predetermined means within a conversation. The process is free-form, and the designer is free to build the client/server conversations in a variety of ways, using any number of data exchanges. In short, except for the specific communication calls required by the transport protocol interface (TCP), there are no rules for implementing client/server computing.

Typically, one service is provided per server, whether it is a data lookup or a data update. The client must already know where the service resides and on what port number the server is listening. This represents a static and limiting situation for LAN administrators on a growing LAN.

RPCs, whether working with DSS or with DNS, ease the burden of building these client/server software products by proceduralizing the development process and by providing a dynamic means of registering and locating the particular service on the network.

Proceduralizing the Development Process   Using the RPC Interface Definition Language (IDL), specific data parameters for the service being provided from the server are coded in the same way a subroutine call defines its arguments in C. This interface definition is read by the IDL compiler, which produces a .h file used by the client and server in providing the service. Additionally, this IDL processor generates the communication calls (sockets) needed by the client and server in order to communicate.

This process then determines what data will be sent, the type of data to be sent, what data will be received, and the type of data to be received. It also determines how the data will be sent and received (socket calls are automatically generated). Using the service becomes as simple as making a subroutine call, with the appropriate application data structures being passed as arguments.

Providing a Dynamic Means of Registering and Locating the Server The server code then becomes the more complicated piece. Upon starting, the server must register itself with the DSS or DNS service. The client automatically looks in the DSS or DNS service to find the server location. The client then connects to the server at runtime (I am oversimplifying here so as not to obscure the benefit with the technical description of the process). In this way, servers can be moved about the network and dynamically addressed by the clients regardless of which machine the servers are running on.

Although this process, once installed, is automatic, the coding of this transparency within the server is complicated (perhaps more so than using a direct socket interface). It does provide a simple means of administering the servers on the network, and RPC coding does trade off the free-form method of designing and developing network services with a specific procedure and design discipline. It also establishes a method for service redundancy and incorporates security considerations within the client/server environment.

Of course, none of this solves the complexities associated with programming the same application on different operating systems, although it does provide a means for communication between different applications on different platforms over TCP/IP.

Probably the biggest benefit from opting for a DCE approach, and perhaps the greatest risk, is that you are buying a solution path for network application interconnectivity and administration.

Sybase Open Server and Open Client (Database-centric)

The Open Server product from Sybase is used to transform two-tier software implementation into three-tier software implementation. The Open Server product, like the Open Client product, is a C/C++ library used by a developer to build applications. In a two-tier architecture,

Sybase Open Client talks directly to Sybase SQL Database Server. Open Server applications typically sit in the middle, receive the communications from Open Client, and do something with them before sending them directly to the SQL server. That something depends on the particular application requirements beyond the two-tier implementation. In some instances this may be additional security requirements.

The Open Server library provides support for SQL statements, Sybase RPCs used to execute a Sybase stored procedure, Registered Procedures (special routines coded by the programmer), and a notification procedure which sends an interrupt from an Open Server implementation to an Open Client implementation.

Open Client library is new with Sybase's system 10.x product. Prior to that, DB-Library was used. Open Client library includes DB-Library for backward compatibility. Open Client uses a standard way of building requests to a server, executing commands, and handling the results from the server. Open Client 10.x has different methods of handling errors and messages from the servers.

Open Client library consists of Client Library, DB-Library, and Net-Library. The CS Library calls are common to both Open Client and Open Server. Discussed in this section are the routines to allocate necessary resources, establish connections, send data, receive data, and deallocate resources.

Typically, an Open Client program will initiate a connection request to the server, receive a response back from the server about the connection, then send a request for services. This request could be in the form of a Registered Procedure command to execute a given routine contained in the Open Server that has been previously coded, or an execution of a stored procedure contained in the SQL server. The SQL server/Open Server runs the request and sends the response back to the requesting client. The requesting client then processes the response.

The Open Client communicates with the Open Server and the SQL server using Sybase's specific protocol called TDS (Tabular Data Stream). The Open Server/Open Client communications protocol is not simple. Therefore, the various calls are often grouped together in the form of APIs callable from Open Client programs. These APIs can be divided into five areas:

1. Communications initialization

2. Application connection

3. Application send

4. Application receive

5. Application disconnect

In fact, these five categories describe the majority of data communication scenarios. Sybase Open Client CS Library, like all communication solutions, implements them very differently. Like most middleware solutions, however, they sit on top of the transport (TCP) layer.

Communications Initialization

These five Sybase defined routines are used to allocate a context structure and install callback handlers. The context structure is used to define the data structure that is to be passed between the client and server programs. The callback handlers are used to define routines to handle errors and information about the communications. For simplicity, these routines can be coded into an API called Application_init.

1. *cs_ctx_alloc.*   The Open Client and Open Server must run under a context. This routine allows the application developers to allocate the necessary data structure and information which define the context.

2. *ct_config().*   Once the context structure has been allocated, then the developer has control in choosing predefined modes and setting different options for the context.

3. *ct_callback().*   Error and informational messages from Open Server and SQL server will be received by the handlers in the Open Client. The Open Client message callback handler receives the messages coming from the servers. The Open Client error callback handler will receive the error messages, which are mainly the result of calling different routines in improper order or the result of syntax error. There are callback handlers to receive notification messages that are coming from other Open Clients via the Open Server.

4. *ct_init.*   Once the context is set, the configuration of this context is completed by the initialization routines, and the callback handlers are installed, the next step is to initialize the Open Client environment with this information.

5. *cs_ctx_drop.*   This routine drops all the resources that have been assigned during the allocation phase, as explained above. This routine is called when the Open Client application exits.

Connection Routines

There are four connection routines defined in CS Library. These routines allocate the context resources to a particular connection, define the properties of a connection, do the connection to the server, and then drop the connection once the service is complete. These are defined in ct_con_alloc, ct_con_props, ct_connect, and ct_con_drop, respectively.

Send Routines

Once the connect routines have executed, the send routines are used to write data across the network to the Open Server application. These Sybase CS library calls set up a particular remote procedure name and execute it.

1. *ct_cmd_alloc.* The Open Client talks to either Open Server or SQL server over a connection. The conversation takes place through something called a *command.* The command is a structure which will contain the name of the command, and a command structure is specified for a connection. The developer uses this routine to allocate the command structure for a specific connection. A connection can contain multiple command structures.

2. *ct_command.* This routine names the command to be sent over the server connection. The command can be a language request, an RPC command, or a Registered Procedure.

3. *ct_parm.* This routine is used when passing the input/output parameters to the RPC and Registered Procedure requests.

4. *ct_send.* This routine actually sends the command and the associated parameters.

Receive Routines

These routines are used to process the row and column data returned by the particular remote procedure executed in the send routines. These Sybase functions include calls to get the number of columns and the description of the column data as well as routines to allocate storage to hold them. These routines include

1. *ct_results.* This routine is used to get the results back from Open Server or SQL server for the previous request sent over the connection.

2. *ct_res_info.* This routine returns metadata. It includes information on the type of data being returned, such as compute results, normal rows, RPC/Registered Procedure, return parameters, etc.

3. *ct_describe.* This routine describes the information about a specific column in the results table. The name, data type, and maximum length are among the data returned by this function.

4. *ct_bind.* This routine sets up local variables in the client routine which are used to contain the results of the fetch command described below.

5. *ct_fetch.* This routine, contained in a loop, is used to fetch the results coming from the server and process them.

Disconnect Routines

Once the client has completed its task, these routines are used to close down the connection to the server and deallocate resources:

1. *ct_close.* This routine closes a connection and deallocates the structure needed for the connection.

2. *ctx_drop.* This routine deallocates the various structures previously allocated in the initialization routines.

MQ Series (Messaging)

MQ series product is one of several different middleware solutions offered by IBM. This product takes advantage of message queues (sometimes file-based, other times transient memory) to store messages from programs. These messages are then read by communications programs operating between platforms to send and receive data. The advantages to the programmer consist of well-defined APIs used to read and write data to the message queues. The communications protocols are transparent. The disadvantage, at least on a UNIX platform, is the need to manage the message queues.

Implementers have found that the use of this product requires development of additional APIs beyond those provided by MQ, which are used by the application programmers.

Implementing a solution using message queues limits the design choices, since it presupposes the use of UNIX message queues as an interprocess communications mechanism when an internal sockets implementation might be better. That aside, the products do offer some help to client/server implementers who need a solution to support asynchronous guaranteed delivery.

There are three basic components of MQ: the queue manager, the message queues themselves, and the APIs used by the program to send and receive messages into and from the message queues.

1. *Queue manager.* Applications obtain message queuing services through the APIs to a local queue manager.

2. *Message queues.* There are six different types of message queues defined by the MQ series: local queues, remote queues, transmission queues, alias queues, model queues, and dynamic queues.

   a. *Local queues.* Local queues belong to the queue manager to which the application has connected via the MQCONN call. Local queues hold messages and are implemented files or in memory.

   b. *Remote queues.* Remote queues belong to a queue manager other than the one to which the application is connected. These queues are opened for output using MQPUT or MQPUT1.

   c. *Transmission queues.* Transmission queues are specialized queues for use by the queue manager and message channel agents. Transmission queues are not accessed directly by normal applications. These queues are used when a local application sends a message to a remote queue. The queue manager places these remote-bound messages on a transmission queue instead of on the local queue. Transmission queues get rather complicated, as there is not just one for each different remote destination—there can be multiple transmission queues for a destination if there are different classes of service for the remote queue.

   d. *Alias queues.* Alias queues simply represent different names for existing queues.

   e. *Model queues.* Model queues are used to define the attributes of a dynamically created queue.

   f. *Dynamic queues.* There are two types of dynamic queues, permanent and temporary. Temporary queues are not recovered if the queue manager fails, nor can persistent messages be put in temporary queues. Permanent dynamic queues are not deleted until an application successfully issues an MQCLOSE call for the queues. Permanent dynamic queues are recovered if the queue manager fails, and persistent messages can be put on them.

As in most middleware solutions, there are six classes of calls:

1. Connecting to the queue manager
2. Opening a message queue
3. Putting a message on the queue
4. Getting a message
5. Closing a message queue connection
6. Disconnecting from a queue manager

IBM with the MQ series, Sybase with Open Client/Open Server, and Open Software Foundation with the DCE specification have each created new and costly job specialties. This summary gives the reader just an idea of the complexities involved in these different solutions.

6

Application Services Addressing

A client that wishes to use an application service requests the network address of the service by using an API which returns the address and the port number where the service is listening for requests (Fig. 6.1). The client then connects to that address and port number. The server program accepts the request and returns a positive acknowledgment to the client that the request is accepted.

A handle is returned which represents the address of the service on the network. This handle is then used by the send command to put data onto the connected service and by the receive verb to get responses from the service. These sends and receives need to be coordinated. The default for these calls is synchronous, but asynchronous versions can be programmed.

Figure 6.1
Network addressing.

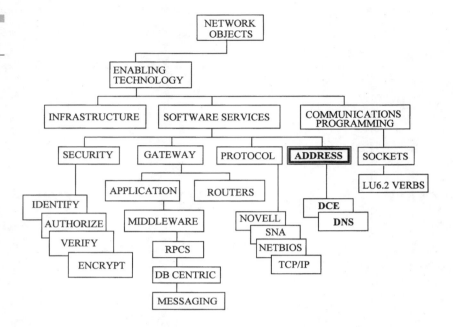

Stream vs. Record

When sockets are used for communication, no application data boundaries are provided to the client program, but special delimiter characters can be included in the stream to delimit application data boundaries.

More often than not, the data being sent to the application server is bound for some other network, such as SNA. Gateways are provided to move the request from the gateway to the SNA service which is its ultimate destination. Different acknowledgments are sometimes required along the way; these are discussed in detail later.

Transparent Data Location

As can be seen in Figs. 6.2 and 6.3, TCP/IP, along with Domain Name Servers, is a basic enabler of transparent data location.

Domains and subdomains are a way of hierarchically arranging networks on networks and nodes on networks. For all domains, root domains begin the hierarchical definition. Other subdomains within the root domain may be organized according to geographical criteria,

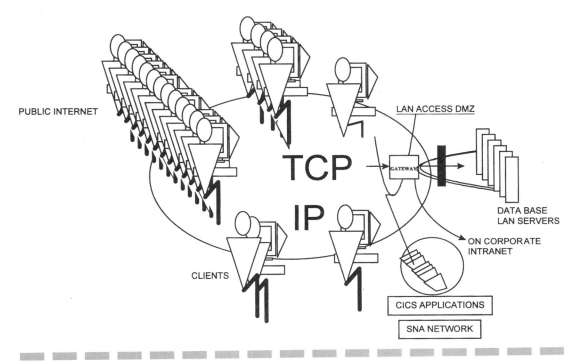

Figure 6.2 Transparent data location.

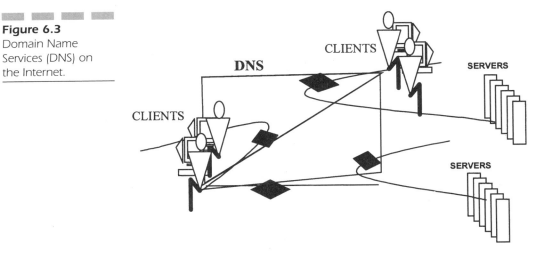

Figure 6.3
Domain Name
Services (DNS) on
the Internet.

along organizational lines, or by other functional groups. Domains represent the way the network administrators view their network and member nodes.

Depending on security requirements, there are a number of different ways to implement this feature. As discussed previously, Domain Name Servers with well-known addresses exist on the network and are available to clients who need to find out the addresses of different servers on the Net.

These servers, known by their IP addresses, also have ordinary English names which get translated into IP addresses. By using API calls like GetHostByName(), the client can send a common English name to a DNS and get a response. The client can then connect to the server's address returned in this response.

Domain Name Services (DNS) provide a list of addresses for application servers and services on the Internet. DNS exist within a domain and provide the IP addresses of all server nodes in the domain. Clients make automatic calls to DNS for name and address resolution.

This works reasonably well for relatively secure LANs where remote node access is not a requirement. In cases where it is, a different approach is needed. When gateways exist on firewalled LANs, the corporate network is secured from access by remote clients. Data servers usually do not exist on the gateway LAN segment which sits outside the firewalled router. Therefore, access to the DNS server is not allowed. Instead, remote users are forced onto a gateway and the gateway acts on behalf of the client to route the request as discussed above (see Fig. 6.2).

Network Security

Firewalled proxy services on a gateway allow corporate customers or external remote access users the ability to access data and request resources from the internal corporate network (see Fig. 7.1). Key to this ability is the use of gateway technology with secure access to internal database servers, whether they are on the SNA network or a local LAN segment someplace.

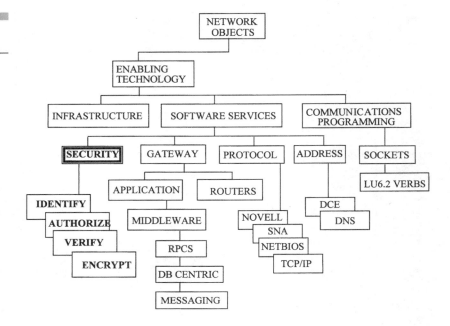

Presented in Fig. 7.2 is an isolated LAN segment which contains the entry point for external users who need to access corporate information resources. Sitting between the two firewalls is the isolated LAN segment containing the gateway. This gateway is the only point of access for a user. Here, firewalls are deployed along with security servers to filter access, validate users, encrypt messages, and offer message authentication services.

There are a number of new products in this area, and the available technology changes rapidly. But the primary reason for a firewall is to limit the number of places on the network a remote user can go, and to have the gateway execute proxy requests on behalf of the client for services available on the network. Available services are limited to the remote client. For example, login sessions, FTP, PING, FINGER, and any number of TCP/IP-based services can be disabled for particular network interfaces.

Security servers are now available which can operate on token technology and provide a reasonable safeguard by authenticating users based on login ID and password. These same security servers allow access to certain services existing on the gateway and then authenticate each message coming into that service to verify that it is from a previously authorized user. These security services exist as API calls between the client

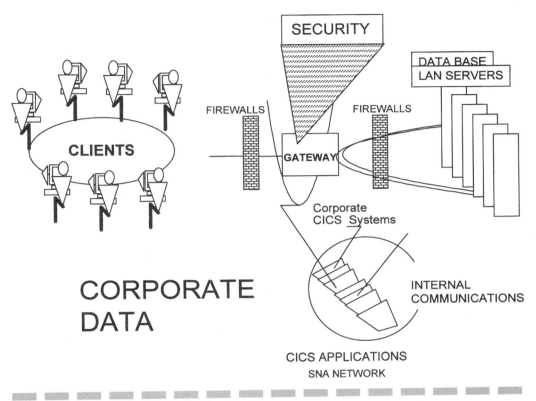

Figure 7.2 Transparent security, single point of access.

application and the server. The security server is configured on the LAN and acts like any other networking software service. It is called by applications which must verify that a particular user is authorized for a certain service.

Network security is probably the fastest-growing concern for corporations extending their networks beyond the traditionally closed campus borders and directly connected WAN technology. The advent of a worldwide network like the Internet and the potential for business expansion and delivery of services to an installed base in the millions, growing faster than anyone can keep up with, has created unparalleled business opportunity. Note the recent appearance of an Internet bank, Security First Network Bank, located at www.sfnb.com. As fast as these opportunities and risks have advanced, the development of new technology to lessen the risk associated with opening the corporate network to external access by customers and telecommuting employees has not been far behind.

Heretofore, the typical network security system was composed of a challenge to the user when the initial connection to the point of access on the network was made. This might be a router or terminal server. Once the challenge response mechanism was effected, the user was cleared into the corporate network onto the platform or server destination.

The typical user request amounted to a switched dial connection to a terminal session through a TTY port, or more recently a Telnet session via TCP/IP/PPP. Once the initial session was secured and the user's identity verified, the user had free rein on the network to perform file transfers, Telnet to other machines on the network, etc. This type of security really amounted to no security and has rapidly changed.

In addition to user verification during the original connect request at the circuit layer, other security options have been put in place to further protect corporate resources from would-be intruders and unauthorized employees.

For example, it is common now to see security in the form of firewalls that filter out only certain IP destinations on the corporate LAN. And those platforms contain only proxy services which act on the behalf of the connected client, at the application layer for other application services on the network.

These proxy services verify that the particular client requester is authorized to request the particular proxy service. At that point, the particular client coming in the network has passed through

- Circuit-level security
- IP filtering layer security
- Session-layer security (port access only)
- Application-layer security on the platform as well

Once it has been confirmed that a client is an authorized user of a particular service, that client can execute only the proxy service that has been made available, and is not able to reach the command operating system environment to issue system-level requests.

While they use certain security standards (a study in itself), Internet security packages do not operate in the same manner. Firewall technology is *proprietary.* One company's client will not work with another company's firewall server even if they both use the same key generation scheme (VeriSign or Nortel's Entrust). So corporations that wish to do business with their customers over the Internet are faced with a multitude of issues. The corporate network needs to be secured, key management and distribution must be set up and maintained, and customer platforms must be configured with security software that does not interfere with existing or future customer network applications.

Securing the Corporate Network

Most plans set up a DMZ (demilitarized zone) network segment. Materially, the DMZ is a separate LAN segment. A firewall sits between the DMZ segment and the rest of the corporate intranet.

The DMZ hosts a gateway machine and a firewall platform. The firewall platform protects the gateway platform from intruders. The firewall is configurable to allow access to only certain proxy services running on the gateway machine. The firewall sitting between the DMZ and the corporate network allows only requests from the proxy services on the gateway to pass through to the rest of the corporate network.

This is a fairly standard configuration. The complexity comes from the method of authentication and verification used between the internet external clients and the firewall protecting the gateway proxy server on the DMZ.

There are two physical configurations available. The first is a LAN-to-LAN system. Two firewalls are used to protect the WAN connection between the two LANs. Nodes on either LAN may attempt connections to acquire resources.

The second physical configuration is remote node protection. Clients run software which connects to a firewall that verifies and authenticates the client machine as a valid network member. This authentication occurs using one of two methods, shared secret keys and public/private keys.

Key Management and Distribution

Keys are used to provide encryption and decryption of the data between the two platforms and to initially authenticate the client. They do not, however, authenticate the user of the PC client. After the platform authentication, the firewall may or may not be configured to send a challenge for user ID and password back to the client.

These keys, whether shared secret or public/private, require management. Key management is often not part of the firewall implementation. The firewalls simply do the authentication, verification, and encryption. Key management issues relate to

1. Generating the public/private key pair used by the client and the firewall.

2. Revoking public/private keys which are compromised in some way.

3. Initially distributing the private keys and tokens generated by them to the clients.

Key assignment and distribution are currently enabled by two different technologies. The first was developed by VeriSign Inc.; this company has Ameritech, Visa, Microsoft, Netscape, and IBM as partners. VeriSign actually assigns the public and private keys used in the authentication process by different firewalls, and mails the keys to the customer.

Nortel, with its Entrust product, allows large corporations to generate public/private key pairs and distribute them via the Internet in a secure manner.

The firewalls and the component pieces (clients) must be enabled to use these two different key management schemes. All firewalls are not created equal.

Firewalls

The simplest and least intrusive firewalling schemes protect LAN-to-LAN connections over WANs. These require no client node configuration and therefore are transparent to the internal networks being protected. Remote node schemes which require setup on the client are more complicated. If the client platforms are Windows 95 or Windows NT, these security implementations are straightforward and operate on the shipped TCP/IP stack. Windows 3.1 and Windows for Workgroups are a different matter, however.

There is no standard TCP/IP for the Windows package, and the different client implementations may or may not work on the third-party TCP/IP vendor's stack. In addition, the security product is usually integrated within a corporation's own access application package. Installation of the security piece and its use should be buried within the setup of the application access package. In addition, the use of the security package should not interfere with other network applications running locally at the client site.

The user/client calls into an external LAN which is firewalled from the corporate LAN via filtering devices that allow only requests from a particular platform. As stated above, these requests are made via proxy services executed on behalf of the client/user. In this configuration, the client is never able to connect directly to any resource running on the corporate network. This particular arrangement places nonintrusive security onto a firewalled external LAN segment on the corporate network and allows only authorized users to enter the firewalled LAN, and then only to execute proxy services that are specific in nature (see Fig. 7.3).

[a] WAN LAN CONNECTION WITH SNA ACCESS

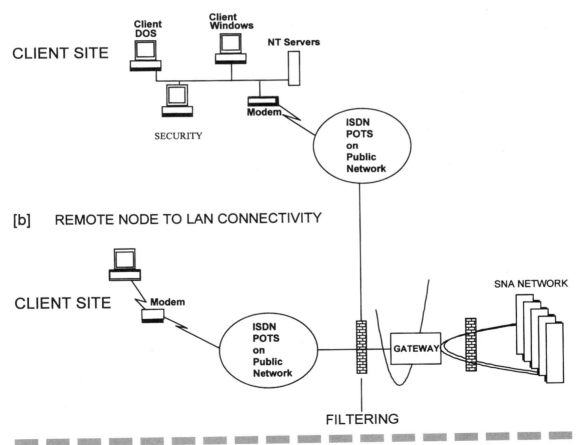

[b] REMOTE NODE TO LAN CONNECTIVITY

Figure 7.3 (a) WAN/LAN connection with SNA access. (b) Remote node–to–LAN connectivity.

Proxy Services

These proxy services may include HTTP servers that get data from behind the firewall or do database access through CGI connections to other databases behind the firewall. Or these proxies may include other TCP/IP requests to forward data to other services that exist behind the firewall and receive responses on behalf of the client, then return the retrieved data to the client. These proxies may also act as application gateways that forward requests from one network to another network via application gateways such as SNA services on the mainframe.

These same proxies then receive the responses and return them to the client requester waiting on the proxy service platform. All other requests are filtered. If the proxy should receive a request from a nonauthorized client, the proxy service would then check for proper message formatting. If it is not correct, the request would be discarded. But these requests are also validated by a security service.

In addition to these configurations that are nonintrusive to the application, there are other forms of security that include the authentication and verification of all messages that flow between client and server programs to verify that messages sent to proxy services are from a previously authorized user, and that the messages being received by the proxy service have arrived unchanged from the originating client.

There are a number of products being developed to secure networks from unauthorized access with the above requirements in mind. These products provide

- Access only to certain platforms on a LAN firewalled from the corporate network

- Access only to proxy services on these certain platforms, which then act to do specific things on behalf of the client

- Authentication by the proxy service that this requester has access privileges to this proxy service

- Verification that the message received by the proxy server is from the authorized client and has arrived untampered

These products are based on two schemes: private key implementations, and newer public/private key implementations. Private key schemes include using a third service sitting on the firewalled proxy service LAN to match tokens between the client and the service being requested. This third service has the job of coordinating the matching of the two pieces of the token to verify identity. For example, when a client wishes to connect to a secured server, the secured server, upon receiving the connection, issues a challenge to the client.

The client must then respond appropriately to the server's challenge or the connection is not made. This is the standard method used to provide point-of-access security. It is usually implemented on top of the communications drivers between the communication devices, but more recent implementations have placed this security check between the two platforms—i.e., security is placed between the platform and the communications device (terminal server or router) or between the two platforms themselves. These schemes are usually implemented below the IP layer (see Fig. 7.4).

Session-layer connections are handled in a similar manner. When the service receives a request for a session from a client which is not part of the internal network, a challenge is made to the incoming client and the client must respond appropriately; otherwise the session is denied.

If the client responds appropriately, then the session is secured. This is usually handled at the TCP/IP layer.

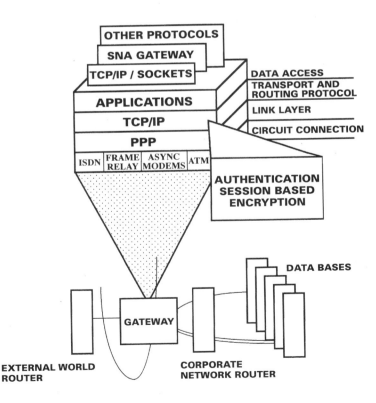

Figure 7.4
Internet gateway security requirements: gateway components enhanced.

Likewise, at the application level, the proxy service being requested by the client calls the security server on the firewalled LAN to verify that the client has been authorized. If the verification fails, the proxy service would deny the connection to the service for the specific user.

Message authentication and verification is implemented in a similar manner. Each message is checked via the keys held in memory from the initial check to ensure that the message has arrived intact. A new set of keys is usually used for each new session.

This challenge-response token technology has taken the form of private keys, where the receiving side must know about the private key of the sender. More recently, challenge-response token technology has used public/private keys, where the receiving side knows only the public key information for a particular user. The private key is known only to the client and is tied to an algorithm.

Upon receiving the private key, the proxy service must contact a public certificate authority to verify that this private key does indeed belong to an authorized user for the system and that the message is from an authenticated user (see Fig. 7.5).

This is accomplished via an algorithm that encrypts the message at the customer site and forwards it over the network to the application proxy service, which receives the message, then verifies that the message is from the authorized session user and has arrived untampered. This is the emerging trend for establishing security over Internet links. Third-party certificate authorities that provide this authentication service are not readily available. Corporations that wish to use this type of scheme to do business may find themselves in the public key certification business if the same client establishes this relationship with another provider who needs to verify public key data.

From the public/private key scheme has come the concept of *digital signature*. Digital signatures accompany each message sent by the user and are a product of the client software and the private key; they uniquely stamp and encrypt the message as being from the user, and the server software public key recognizes that the message is from this user and has arrived untampered. This security is implemented at the proxy service layer.

Because the service provider does not know the client's private key, this form of digital signature gives the service provider nonrefutable evidence that the message received was from the client; if the message turns out not to have been sent by the client, then it was the client that compromised security, not the service provider. This nonrefutability is not available in private key schemes.

Figure 7.5
Gateway proxy ser-
vices enhanced and
shown in session
with client.

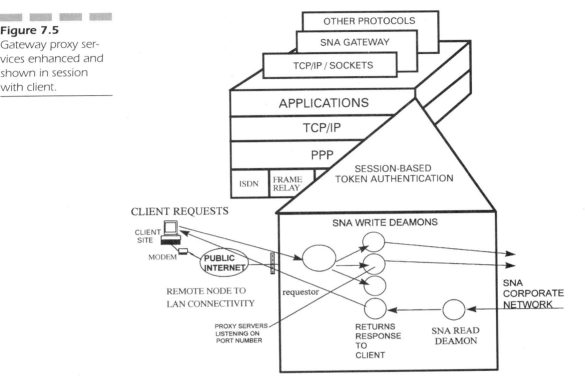

Private key schemes involve the service provider's knowing the client's key and resolving the match of the client's key with another private key held by the service provider. This is usually referred to as *shared secrets*. The same authentication processes described above take place, but in this case the two shared secrets, the contents of the message via an algorithm, resolve to some common random number. If the numbers don't match, then the data has changed or the message is from another user.

For both private and public key systems, there are ANSI standards which dictate how the systems are implemented. Innumerable volumes have been written about these particular standards, and they are constantly being developed and refined.

There are a number of companies participating in the evolution of security products. Some offer only basic circuit-layer security. Others offer a combination of session-layer and application-layer security. Some offer encryption algorithms and others do not, and some offer message verification and authentication.

Many of these products are based on software-only solutions; others include hardware and are placed on the LAN that is being protected.

Most comply with the ANSI standards that have been or are being developed. Nearly all offer a software token used by the client or smart card hardware that requires the user to enter a series of ever-changing numbers in order to be cleared into a protected network. This solution, however, has not proved very popular with users.

To secure a client/server connection, the user initially loads the particular security product onto the PC. On the very first invocation of the security piece, the software realizes that it has no key, connects to the security server at its known address, and performs a secure key exchange. In addition to the various layers of security, most of these products provide a log which records all attempts at access, successful or otherwise, so that intruders can be detected. In addition, most of these products provide a mutual challenge response.

The digital signatures are X.509 standard certificates based on an RSA public key, and they are evolving into a super secure method of identifying clients, as previously discussed. Because responsibility for the security rests with the client, many banks and brokerage firms plan to deploy this form of security. A certificate by itself is useful for authentication and key exchange, but it does not permit storage of additional useful information, such as electronic cash or access rights. Processing these certificates requires the use of software APIs built into the client and server software to provide signature and certificate verification (third party).

Another form of security that involves granting tokens, adopted by OSF, HP, DEC, and IBM, is the KERBOROS authentication service. The current version, version 5, has become the de facto standard for network authentication. The KERBOROS service provides a third-party key distribution center that authenticates clients to different network services. Such a service allows networks to be secured by one trusted third party. A service provides tokens that identify different network client entities as required; any two network entities can communicate as long as each trusts the source of the tokens. Also, a key distribution center distributes these keys to those with proven identities. Such a service must be on a very secure defensible platform.

Summary

Authentication is the first of three primary tools to protect against attack; the others are authorization and auditing. Additional tools include nonreputation, privacy, and integrity. All the security tools which authenticate users for a given proxy service or application work at the application layer in the OSI stack. Therefore, these solutions require that calls be embedded within the proxy service to communicate with a security service, which ultimately grants the proxy service authority to validate the user for that service.

Inherent in these solutions is a three-tier proxy architecture. The client never talks directly to the server, but is represented to the application server by a proxy server. This limits the ability of current technologies to authenticate two-tier client/server applications. At this writing, most major database vendors are enhancing the SQL server product to include user and message authentication and verification.

The existing LAN gateway implementation, through the use of proxy services and firewalls, protects the corporate LAN from direct external access. Assuming that this proxy service architecture is extended as a way of doing business with external users, then the security discussions currently under discussion are to

1. Protect the proxy application on the gateway from unauthorized use.

2. Verify that all messages received by the gateway are from an authorized user and that the messages arrived intact.

3. Provide event logging for all access into the network.

Public Internet

The public Internet is a good example of a network which is composed of all the objects discussed in the previous chapters. It is useful to look at because of its growing popularity and the benefits which the infrastructure and software services can provide to corporations placing applications (content) there. This chapter provides a basic overview of this infrastructure and the existing software services used by the corporate intranet.

Chapter 7, "Network Security," explains how the corporate network is protected from unauthorized users but at the same time allows authorized users of the Internet to access corporate data.

What Is the Internet?

The Internet is a worldwide network of networks, with gateways linking organizations in North and South America, Europe, the Pacific Basin, and other countries. It has no central worldwide control point. Nonetheless, cooperation has enabled it to be viewed by users as a single virtual global network.

Corporate intranets and the worldwide Internet, though based on the same technology, are in fact completely different, albeit compatible, entities. This is one of the ironies about the Internet that can be confusing. The Internet is a worldwide network of networks that can include any number of different private corporate intranets.

The other confusing thing about the Internet is that there is no central worldwide control point. Each member is responsible for managing its particular section of the Internet. Nonetheless, through cooperation, a single virtual user network has been created. This is the most compelling reason for corporations to use it to extend services.

Internet History

The Internet began as a Department of Defense experiment in 1969. In 1984, there were over 1000 computers on the Internet. By mid 1995 there were over 6 million interconnected platforms. This number continues to grow monthly. In fact, nobody really knows how many different users there are on the Internet.

Internet Access

Access to the Internet is provided by commercial Internet service providers (ISPs), on-line service providers (OSPs), and more and more telecommunications carriers. Most users connect to one of the Internet providers through either dial-up lines, ISDN, or leased lines.

It is important to distinguish between the Internet service providers and the on-line service providers. As a rule, on-line service providers use a form of terminal proprietary protocol to connect customers and provide a gateway to the public Internet.

Commercial Internet providers, however, connect users directly to the public Internet. The difference here is that software developed to run on the commercial Internet via client/server interfaces will not run over on-line service connections, but will run properly over a commercial Internet service provider. Therefore, companies that wish to extend the client/server paradigm developed in the previous chapters would be able to do so with a commercial Internet service provider, but could not do so with an on-line service provider.

Internet Services

The Internet provides a variety of entertainment, daily news, communications, education, etc.:

- Communication, education, broadcast media, daily news, booklike materials
- Advertising, want ads, magazine and direct market retailing, banking
- Through the World Wide Web, e-mail, file transfer, Usenet
- Future: video, audio, telephony, conferencing, collaborative work

There is tons of advertising, such as want ads and direct marketing, on the Internet. Recently an Internet bank has appeared. The Internet technology which has created this synergy between infrastructure and software is based on World Wide Web technology and e-mail. The future of the Internet is in video and audio conferencing. It will include collaborative work environments as well as provide a means for delivering multimedia technology.

Internet Service Providers vs. On-line Service Providers

As previously mentioned, Internet service providers and on-line service providers give users different types of service. There are over 3000 Internet service providers with local, regional, and Internet access.

Internet Service Providers

These service providers all include dial-up IP access to the providers' network. TCP/IP SLIP or PPP exists on every client using an IP service provider and on every server wishing to use the provider as a transport mechanism for deployed applications. All sessions are real-time.

Advantages to using an Internet service provider include nationwide access from local numbers, lower charges, direct use of the WWW, and the ability to host private client/server software over the network connections. This alone is a significant advantage for clients who wish to extend their services over the Net without the added cost of creating another physical network.

On-line Provider Access

Attributes of on-line provider access are as follows:

- Access is easy (but the network is proprietary, not TCP).
- Each network is different, with limited offerings.
- Most have dial-up access servers throughout the country.
- Servers are interconnected on a proprietary network.
- They do not host private client/server applications.

To be sure, on-line provider access has its benefits. But these mostly accrue to private users who want to take advantage of application services available to subscribers, rather than to corporations looking for a means of extending services to clients.

Following the network nomenclature scheme developed in Chap. 1, the Internet is composed of three primary classes: the infrastructure, software and services, and the content (see Fig. 8.1). This chapter differs from the last three in that the discussion of software and services will include a detailed discussion of the use of Hypertext Transport Protocol (HTTP) servers for delivery of services to clients.

Internet Components

The Internet is a tiered organization that consists of three parts:

1. Network access providers

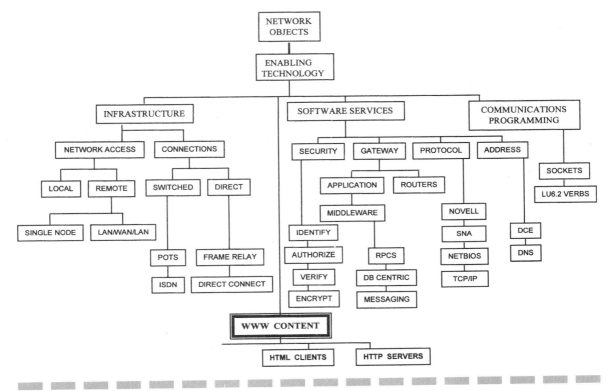

Figure 8.1 Public Internet components.

2. Network service providers

3. High-speed backbone

Network access providers exist in four regions of the country: California, Chicago, Washington, D.C., and New York. The network access providers give the network service providers like Netcom, UUNET, and PSI access to the Internet backbone, top layer, managed by MCI (see Figs. 8.2 and 8.3). As the map illustrates and the organization chart depicts, the Internet is a tiered network with multiple member communities on each tier.

Local network providers give users dial-in access to a network. These networks, in turn, connect to the network access providers. The network access providers then provide entry into the high-speed backbone. In this way, users from all parts of the country may access any other point on the connected Internet, whether in the United States or worldwide, with a local phone call.

Figure 8.2
Internet organization.

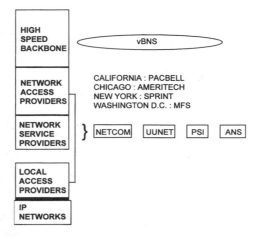

Figure 8.3
Tiered access to the Internet in the United States.

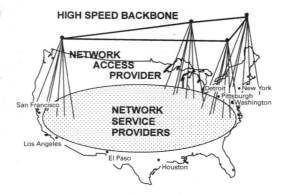

Software and Services

The software and services component of the Internet is very similar to that of the corporate intranet discussed earlier in the book. It is all based on TCP/IP protocols, which allow clients from any point to access servers on any other point in the connected Internet world. The clients and servers both must access, as discussed previously, via IP address and services running on particular port numbers on those IP-addressed platforms. As there are millions of clients accessing hundreds of thousands of services on the Internet at any moment in time, an addressing scheme to determine the address of a particular service is needed.

Domain Name Services   The Domain Name Service (DNS) is a global service provided on the Internet that enables any client anywhere in the world to find the address of any server or service hooked up to the Internet (see Fig. 8.4). DNS provides a list of addresses for applications servers and services on the Internet. Domain Name Servers exist in a domain and contain the IP address of all servers on the Internet. DNS also holds the addresses of other DNS *if the IP address is not listed.* Clients make automatic calls to DNS for IP address name resolution without realizing they have done so.

This scheme is the basis for the primary technology that has made Internet access so uniform. Through the WWW, a common access protocol has been developed and is now used on the Internet. The WWW consists of Hypertext Markup Language documents (HTMLs) which contain information about subjects that users view (see Fig. 8.5). Uniform Resource Locators (URLs) contain the addresses of HTTP servers and other codes. These HTTP servers are accessed via a URL. These servers then, in turn, access the HTML pages the client is interested in. The client is able to access and read the HTML information via a variety of browsers. Netscape is the most common.

In addition to providing access to HTML documents containing information, HTTP servers can, through the use of a Common Gateway Interface (CGI), provide proxy access to other database resources on the corporate internet. Through network browsers, users can query Sybase, Oracle, or other corporate databases via HTTP proxy services.

Figure 8.4
Domain Name Services (DNS) and addresses on the Internet.

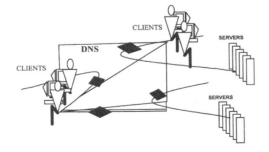

- PROVIDE A LIST OF ADDRESSES FOR APPLICATION SERVERS AND SERVICES ON THE INTERNET.

- DOMAIN NAME SERVERS EXIST WITHIN A DOMAIN AND PROVIDE THE IP ADDRESSES OF ALL SERVER NODES IN THE DOMAIN.

- CLIENTS MAKE AUTOMATIC CALLS TO DNS FOR NAME ADDRESS RESOLUTION.

Figure 8.5
World Wide Web.

- HTML (HYPER TEXT MARKUP LANGUAGE) DOCUMENTS

- URLS (UNIFORM RESOURCE LOCATORS)

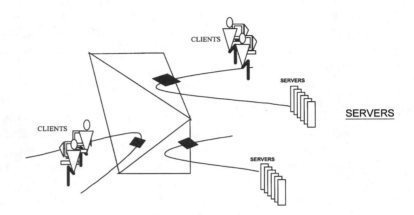

But it is in fact the URLs that allow WWW browser clients to indicate the target server and specify Internet resources (see Fig. 8.6). The URL protocol contains a protocol to use when accessing a server, such as the HTTP, e-mail, and Internet domain name of the site on which the service is running, the port number of the resource, and a string argument if it is HTTP URL.

Functions of the URL are as follows:

1. Allows WWW browser clients to indicate the target of the hypertext links.
2. Specifies Internet resources.
3. Contains the protocol to use when accessing server HTTP, Gopher, or WAIS.
4. Provides the Internet domain name of the site on which the server is running.
5. Supplies the port number.
6. Furnishes the location of the resource in the hierarchy structure of the server.
7. Creates the string argument for an HTTP URL.

- HTML (HYPER TEXT MARKUP LANGUAGE) DOCUMENTS
- HTTP (HYPER TEXT TRANSPORT PROTOCOL) SERVERS
- URLS (UNIFORM RESOURCE LOCATORS)
- CGI (COMMON GATEWAY INTERFACE)

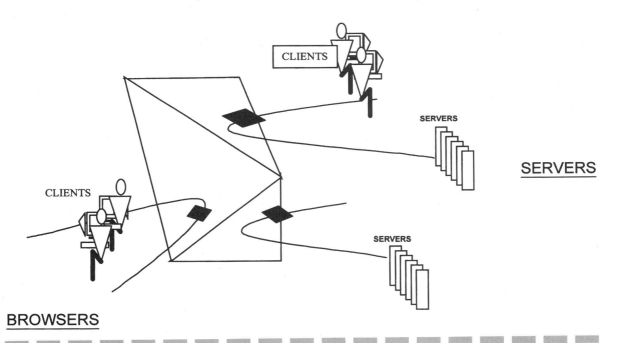

Figure 8.6 URL function.

Internet Communication

Furthermore, the Internet provides three types of communication. In addition to the URL WWW access, there is Telnet access for terminal protocol, so that users may dial in, connect to a system, and issue commands to the operating systems via some shell; File Transfer Protocol (FTP), used in copying and sending files between different nodes; and On-Line Transaction Protocols (OLTP) similar to HTTP, where users access clients that communicate with services like those described in the corporate intranet chapters (see Fig. 8.7).

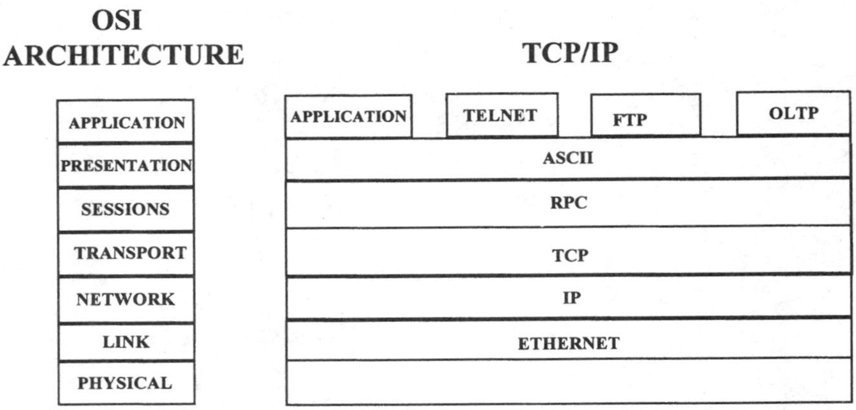

Figure 8.7
Three types of communication: Telnet, FTP, and OLTP.

OSI ARCHITECTURE

TCP/IP

OSI ARCHITECTURE	TCP/IP
APPLICATION	APPLICATION TELNET FTP OLTP
PRESENTATION	ASCII
SESSIONS	RPC
TRANSPORT	TCP
NETWORK	IP
LINK	ETHERNET
PHYSICAL	

The TCP/IP and gateway diagram (Fig. 8.8) illustrates where applications actually sit on the Internet network and how routers and gateways enable universal Internet access. Network service providers and local access providers host these different protocols and gateways that enable communication between themselves and the network access providers.

Finally, the Internet has two potential benefits to corporations in the current market:

1. It is potentially useful as a network transport provider.

2. World Wide Web browsers can be used as clients to assess databases.

First, the Internet is a readily available transport provider that can host custom-built client/server applications which communicate over the existing public Internet to provide long-distance customers instant access to corporate resources. This has tremendous potential benefit for banking and other financial services. Second, the WWW, URL, HTTP, and browser technologies available from the Internet provide corporations with built-in clients and servers that enable the immediate participation and dissemination of different types of information from commercially available off-the-shelf software.

Clients with CGI capabilities are able to pass URL requests to back-end database servers such as Sybase and Oracle, receive responses from those servers, and forward them over the Internet to the requesting client (see Fig. 8.9).

One of the most interesting aspects of this architecture is that changes to the client service are made at the server, in one place. Presentation logic is then picked up by the browser the next time a request for

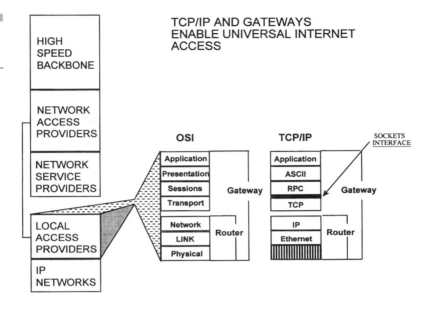

Figure 8.8
TCP/IP and gateway diagram.

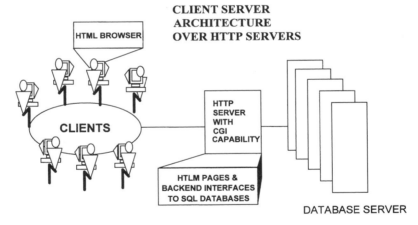

Figure 8.9
Clients using browsers over existing Internet resources to talk to HTTP resources.

the server resource is made. This eliminates maintenance programming and distribution of those changes to clients.

The biggest risk, which heretofore has limited the use of the public Internet as a transport vehicle enabling client/server applications to access corporate stores, has been the security risk associated with such deployment. As in all applications, the design of security within the architecture is of paramount importance. Unlike traditional client/server implementations, which operate in a closed environment, if the security aspects of an application using the Internet are not considered, the application can be impossible to deploy. Chapter 7 discusses the latest thinking concerning firewalling of private networks from users of the public Internet, yet allowing authorized users access to the data on the corporate LAN. This is done by setting up multilevel security devices from the circuit layer to the routing layer, and finally in the proxy application itself.

MVS Application Gateway Architecture and the Team to Build It

This chapter is divided into two parts. The first part discusses the architecture for a gateway project, and the second part discusses the technical management and personnel needed to implement a multiprotocol gateway to access back-end legacy resources.

Application Gateway Architecture

With the prevalence of multiprotocol routers, the emerging picture of a corporate network looks much like Fig. 9.1. As shown, any number of LAN protocols are internetted on a single backbone through various protocol routers. This chapter suggests that, as in the picture in Fig. 9.1, these corporate backbone internets now offer enough interoperability to provide Internet services. The configuration suggested here is mainframe gateway servers accessing legacy systems from any local LAN on the Internet.

Demand for local LAN connectivity to mainframe legacy systems can be satisfied as a corporate internet service with accompanying network management software, load balancing paradigms, and various other network economies. The back-end gateway requires a corporatewide, reusable solution for customer LAN-to-mainframe access.

Providing corporate internet services is of particular interest. The alternative is the current proliferation of local LANs, each with its own service. This creates all the havoc and skyrocketing costs associated with providing duplicate services from different platforms.

Figure 9.1
LAN protocols internetted on a single backbone.

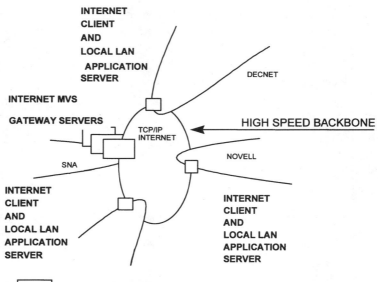

INTERNET
CLIENT
AND
LOCAL LAN
 APPLICATION
SERVER

DECNET

INTERNET MVS

GATEWAY SERVERS

TCP/IP
INTERNET

HIGH SPEED BACKBONE

NOVELL

SNA

INTERNET
CLIENT
AND
LOCAL LAN
APPLICATION
SERVER

INTERNET
CLIENT
AND
LOCAL LAN
APPLICATION
SERVER

NOTE | BOXES DENOTE PROTOCOL ROUTERS

Current Problem

Because the demand for mainframe access from the LAN-based application seeks solutions locally, several expensive problems can occur as the number of requirements for LAN access to mainframe data proliferates. Duplicate costs can include:

1. A proliferation of point-to-point lines from the mainframe to the various "application servers."

2. Addition of new and different platforms on the network to host the gateways.

3. New and different "connectivity software gateway products" on the LAN/WAN network.

4. New development costs each time a LAN connection is required.

5. Escalating maintenance costs associated with these new products, new software gateways, and new network connections.

6. Network management problems with system availability consequences.

7. Providing for gateway redundancy and balancing traffic through the various gateways, which is very expensive, if not prohibitive, without a planned Internet service deployment.

I will now specify the particulars of the above situations.

1. *A proliferation of point-to-point lines from the mainframe to the various "application servers."* In many instances, gateway applications are provided to the LAN application server locally. At the same time, these LANs often are not on a token ring network and require point-to-point service from the gateway to the mainframe. These point-to-point lines increase costs each time such a line is implemented; these costs include setting up the line, buying the DSUs, extra port assignment on the front-end processor, and maintenance. Though these are not problems when one or two are required, the addition of a half dozen or more 56-kbps or 9.6-kbps lines can be very expensive and wasteful when compared to a corporate internet solution.

2. *Addition of new and different platforms on the network to host the gateways.* With every platform vendor and many different software connectivity companies offering dissimilar gateway products for mainframe connections, the user has a wide range of platforms to choose from. Windows versions exist, OS/2 versions exist, and UNIX PCs have their own version

as well. Sun, HP, and RS6000 all have mainframe access products. Application connectivity is all over the place. This is both good and bad for the corporate network.

Because the user on the local LAN seeks mainframe connectivity locally, any number of these products and platforms can be configured to operate as a gateway. And in large organizations with lots of different options, they already exist. Duplication and maintenance of these platforms is difficult. Trying to maintain connectivity and troubleshoot these different platform solutions can be troublesome for a network management group.

With this scenario, each new LAN application needing mainframe access is a new development project and a new maintenance concern, and leads to increasing costs to simply repeat an existing network service for each instance of a local LAN—to—mainframe application. This is particularly true because each platform vendor offers different solutions for the same functionality, mainframe access. These include different ways of implementing the LU6.2 capability and the 3270 terminal emulation products.

3. *New and different "connectivity software gateway products" on the LAN/WAN network.* As alluded to above, these different solutions carry with them different gateway product implementations for the same functionality. All of them have one thing in common, however. They must be configured on the host platform, configured to match the mainframe, and they require development of software communications to their own application program interfaces (APIs).

None of these tasks are particularly simple. They require some expertise in SNA protocols, knowledge of the operating system on the particular platform, knowledge of vendor gateway products, and communications software development.

Repeating any one of these tasks for the same platform can be difficult enough, but repeating one of them for multiple vendor platforms and multiple products can be overwhelming and very costly for even the best-financed organization.

4. *New development costs each time a LAN connection is required.* Given the situation described above, the organization must finance a new development effort every time a LAN user wants to access mainframe data. This involves the tasks outlined above, the development of new code to test the connections, tying up mainframe resources to do testing, and the testing of application software using the new connection.

5. *Escalating maintenance costs associated with these new products, new software gateways, and new network connections.* It is obvious by now that many duplications of different implementations of these gateways are going to be a maintenance problem. New product specialties, new communications software, and new application APIs all need looking after. What may not be so obvious is the ability to manage these different application connections over the different gateway implementations.

6. *Network management problems with system availability consequences.* At the level of conversation between different platforms, communication software failure can occur which is not detected until the application attempts to use it. By then it is too late. Intervention is postactive, not proactive. Most gateway implementation software and communication programs do not address this problem. The user gets notified at the time the application, not the communication, fails.

Creating multiple implementations with different types of local LAN mainframe connectivity solutions is likely to keep things this way. While the user waits to do the work, diagnostic and product specialist teams associated with each different LAN implementation will be needed to address emerging problems. If there are only two or three different implementations, there is not much cause for concern. If there are a half dozen or more, an automated method of proactive intervention, on behalf of the conversation level, within a consistent architecture needs to be developed (next section).

7. *Providing for gateway redundancy and balancing traffic through the various gateways, which is very expensive, if not prohibitive, without a planned Internet service deployment.* The final point here examines gateway service redundancy and load balancing. In the examples above, where the assumption is demand satisfaction locally on the LAN for mainframe connections, the only alternative for redundancy is two of everything.

This means that two gateway platforms, two point-to-point lines, two gateway products networked to SNA, two copies of the communications software, and a means for switching between the two will be required. Even if redundancy is sought on the same platform (e.g., two communication lines), careful implementation is required, and some method of switching between the two is still needed.

This switching software makes it more difficult to use the backup on a daily basis as an additional connectivity pipe, so the backup is often idle until it is required. This results in a blatant waste of expensive network resources.

The Solutions

The architecture proposed in this chapter eliminates these problems and minimizes cost by providing:

1. Mainframe LAN access as an internet service accessible by any number of clients on the internet

2. A common application program interface to permit reusability of communications software across a number of different client platforms

3. Gateway product transparency so that one gateway vendor product may service all TCP/IP internet clients

4. Application network management

5. Load balancing and gateway redundancy on the internet

Now let us further examine the above solutions.

1. *Mainframe LAN access as an internet service accessible by any number of clients on the internet.* This architecture provides for single servers (backup and multiple servers are added as traffic requires) acting as gateways to the mainframe on the platform of choice. All clients providing access to the service are located on the local LAN along with the LAN application needing the mainframe data.

As shown in Fig. 9.1, while using the same internet service, this architecture allows local LANs to provide for a variety of different application environments and local LAN protocols. As noted in Fig. 9.2, the internet client on the local LAN uses a TCP/IP connection to establish sessions over the internet with the intended internet service (mainframe access in this case).

With such a strategy, a single internet mainframe access service can accommodate different application LAN servers and different platforms that may exist on the various local LANs.

2. *A common application program interface to permit reusability of communications software across a number of different client platforms.* Figure 9.2 shows such a scenario, where the client API based on the TCP/IP transport-layer interface (sockets or TLI) is consistent whether the application is in a Windows, Sun UNIX, HP UNIX, or VMS environment. As shown in Fig. 9.2, each of these client platforms can perform two functions: First, it may host the local LAN application services, and second, it acts as an internet client to the access service host (see Fig. 9.1) through a common client communications API.

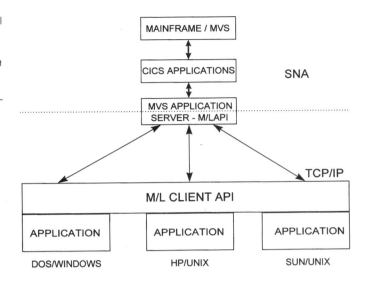

Figure 9.2
Consistent application interface across a variety of TCP/IP host platforms.

This capability gives the LAN user the same mainframe access as a gateway server on the client host would give, without the duplication and cost. No matter which platform is chosen as the application server and the internet MVS client, the API is the same.

The internet server, in turn, becomes the user's platform of choice and hosts the gateway software (which is used by all TCP/IP clients) to the mainframe legacy systems. Because the client is using a TCP/IP standard API for communication with the MVS gateway server, and the gateway server contains the vendor product API front-ended by a standard TCP/IP connection, only one gateway vendor product is required, and only one mainframe-to-server connection is needed (see Fig. 9.3). Contrast this to the need for one mainframe connection for each gateway hosted on the local LAN.

3. *Gateway product transparency so that one gateway vendor product may service all TCP/IP internet clients.* SNA gateway products generally consist of two parts. The first part is the translator from the LAN protocol (TCP/IP, for example) to the SNA stack. This is usually implemented as a server.

The second part of the gateway provides connectivity to the server from a user-specified client. It is this client piece that is written to provide the application-to-application connectivity. Unfortunately, these two pieces, the client piece and the server piece, are not interchangeable among vendors.

For example, Sun's SUNLINK peer-to-peer client cannot use the HP version of the SNA server. Although there are independent implementa-

Figure 9.3
Mainframe gateway
illustration.

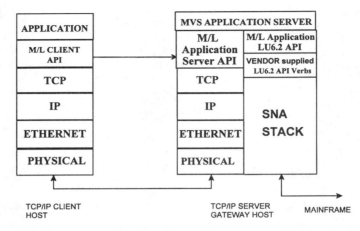

tions of these SNA gateways that cross platforms, their availability on specific hardware is up to the vendor.

This incompatibility among gateway products is not problematic until multiple clients running on different vendor hosts are required. When this occurs, it is not possible to use the same product unless it has been specifically architected to run on different host clients to the specific SNA server. This means that for each different host implementation, a different gateway product with its own mainframe connections would be implemented.

As noted, the problem is caused by incompatibility between the client and server pieces of the specific vendor implementations.

To eliminate this problem, the internet server contains the client piece of the gateway vendor product and the vendor gateway server. Thus the *mainframe server* on the internet actually becomes a client to the gateway product (Fig. 9.3) by using the vendor API client calls.

This creates a transparency between the vendor gateway and the actual client/server implementation on the internet. However, it also requires the additional implementation of a client TCP/IP protocol—based API that runs on the local LAN and communicates with the mainframe server on the internet. This same mainframe server then becomes the client to the vendor gateway and routes the request from the local LAN client to the specific legacy system.

In this way, the vendor-supplied client piece is replaced by client/server which sits in front of the vendor product on the mainframe server.

Figure 9.3 depicts the way internet client and server host platforms could be configured to provide transparent access to mainframe legacy applications through an internet server. In this case, the mainframe access is through the LU6.2 internet service provider.

This particular configuration has a number of advantages:

- The SNA product exists on one host.
- Mainframe access is treated like any other network service [i.e., provided through a gethostbyname( ) call].
- The connectivity product, LU6.2 in this case, is transparent to the client application.
- The connectivity product is transparent to the server application.

Both transparency issues (client and server calls) are addressed by providing a higher-level interface to the lower-level calls, TCP on the client and LU6.2 on the server, so that regardless of protocol, the library of communication services can be utilized. Although this example shows LU6.2 as the access service, Fig. 9.4 shows that any number of different legacy mainframe services, including Seqnet, tn3270, and terminal emulation, could be provided in a similar manner.

At the same time as this architecture eliminates needless duplication in the network, it also sets the stage for a resource balancing and manage-

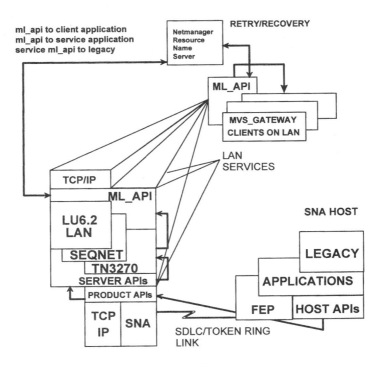

Figure 9.4
Multiple mainframe legacy services.

ment paradigm that facilitates redundancy in the network and provides application network management information for proactive management.

4. *Application network management.* With this architecture, if more than one platform is required to provide the particular access service to the client applications, the network resource manager depicted in Fig. 9.4 is used to provide load balancing on the network.

The internet client uses a gethostbyname( ) call to get the address of the network resource manager, establish the connection with it, request the access service name, then receive the next session channel available to the requested access service.

5. *Load balancing and gateway redundancy on the internet.* Meanwhile, the network manager piece constantly assures availability of the service connections on the internet and the back-end legacy systems. Any abnormal situations are reported to a designated userid/console for corrective action. This architecture thereby enables proactive network application monitoring.

Finally, because this architecture uses asynchronous conversation for its sessions between TCP/IP clients and between the mainframe access server and the mainframe, it can provide flexible configurations without concern for the underlying protocol complexities (see Fig. 9.5).

For example, there can be many clients for one service, and one client may request multiple service. Not shown, but definitely implied, is the fact that many clients may talk to many servers.

Figure 9.5
Flexible session com-
munications.

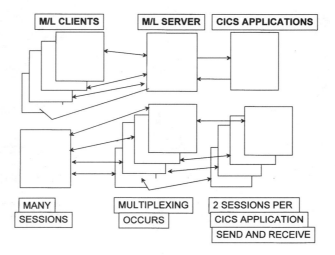

M/L CLIENTS   M/L SERVER   CICS APPLICATIONS

MANY SESSIONS   MULTIPLEXING OCCURS   2 SESSIONS PER CICS APPLICATION SEND AND RECEIVE

Gateway Management Team and Objectives

The departmental and technical interrelationships required to produce integrated systems that include LAN-based applications and mainframe applications are a relatively new phenomenon for most corporate cultures. Methodologies and considerations for developing LAN-based applications and host applications are worlds apart, but the evolution of communication environments designed to cross these worlds and produce integrated systems is bringing them closer together than before.

The networking, planning, and interrelationship of the complex and varied skills needed to produce communication bridges between these technologies is making new demands on old organizational boundaries and blurring the distinction between networks and applications using those networks. The need for new strategies to manage this varied matrix of skills and enable them to work in unison is increasing. Achieving such a strategy will require organizational flexibility and interaction not required of traditional computing solutions.

If business solutions needing these integrated technologies are to be achieved in a cost-effective and beneficial manner, not only will an understanding of the layers of the network architecture be required, but the way this architecture is supported within the organization must also be understood. Management strategies for deploying these types of projects will be as challenging as the deployment of the technology itself. For example, developing an LU6.2 gateway from a local LAN to access corporate data stored on a mainframe seems like a relatively simple undertaking. But the implementation of the concept can be as challenging organizationally as it is technically.

The number of departments and players needed to build and design a point-to-point circuit from a gateway hosting LAN terminals and to actually implement the cooperative application using the circuit can be surprising. To accomplish this, one person must coordinate and own the entire LU6.2 connectivity project, from the physical layer up to the application layer. This person is usually by default the one who wants to connect to the mainframe from the LAN. Personnel required to accomplish this connectivity and the roles they play include

1. Data communications planner

2. Data tech/circuit vendor

3. NCP analyst

4. VTAM analyst

5. CICS programmer

6. CICS systems programmer

7. LAN administrator

8. LAN SNA product specialist

9. Mainframe database specialist

10. LAN database specialist

11. End-user representative

Should any one of these people fail to perform his or her part successfully, the project will not succeed. Should any debugging be required, it may or may not require additional personnel, such as the hardware vendor for the FEP and the hardware/software vendor for the LAN gateway.

An unhappy state of events, such as an unstable link layer, will require a telephone conference between three or four of the persons mentioned above. This will usually be initiated by the LAN SNA product specialist, as this is the person who wants connectivity.

To begin this process of building the link, a data communications planner must OK the link and designate the kind of circuit. Of particular importance is whether this connectivity is considered "new" and placed on the test communications front end, or standard and placed on the production front end. This requires coordination between the FEP system person and the data communications circuit planner. The importance of this decision for future development cannot be overstated. Once development and testing of the link is under way, should that testing point out the need for tuning the link between the LAN platform and the front-end processor (which requires changing NCP parameters), delays caused by the need to schedule the implementation of these parameter changes on a production front end can seriously impede the project.

Additionally, the speed of the circuit and the availability of ports on the FEP can delay the process. Usually low-speed 9.6-kbps links are more available than 56-kbps or higher links.

Once these items have been negotiated, it is necessary to contact a vendor (internal or external) to provide the actual wire between the two points. Once the wire is complete and plugged into the DSU, a point-to-point test is run to ensure the validity of the circuit. Next, the definition of the circuit to the current SNA network architecture is required. This definition takes place via an NCP gen for the front-end processor and a VTAM gen for SSCP specifically. This process will require at least two separate people, the VTAM analyst and the NCP analyst. On the LAN gateway, a third person is involved to work with the VTAM and NCP analysts to coordinate the definitions required for the LAN platform.

The LAN platform generally will host some kind of vendor-provided software which will be loaded by the LAN administrator and set up by a person familiar with both SNA and the LAN-based technology. The same person who sets up the link may also code the LU6.2 verbs on the gateway side.

On the partner mainframe, a CICS programmer and CICS system person will be responsible for coding the application verbs and designating the application to VTAM as LU6.2-capable. Before any coding can begin, it is important to clearly designate the purpose of the link and what application considerations will come into play. Usually a mainframe database is accessed, and often a local LAN database is used to support applications running on the LAN. This generally will require joint meetings involving a different set of people. This group will consist of

1. SNA product specialist on the LAN side

2. SNA CICS programmer

3. DB/2 person

4. LAN database administrator

5. End-user representative

Coordination of the various functions of the distributed application is then determined, and various roles and tasks are assigned to these team members. As the reader may notice, the LAN product specialist and the CICS programmer are common to the data communications group and the applications group. It is important that these two people have a good idea of what is going on with regard to both the communication issue and the application issues and business problem to be solved.

Given this mix of highly specialized and technical people, it is necessary to structure tasks and develop teams to work as independently as possible. The teams consist of:

- CICS DB/2 application team
- Data communication team
- LAN applications group

Because these three teams cut across organizational boundaries and technologies in a way heretofore not experienced, a coordinator who can bring about strategies necessary to accomplish the business objective will be required. The primary goal of such a strategy is, first, to minimize the interdependencies within the groups and, second, to schedule resources concurrently when this is possible, with an understanding of the dependencies of each group's requirements on any other group.

For example, the CICS DB/2 application team will work independently of the LAN application team under a set of specifications which will be bridged by the data communications team, specifically, the CICS communications programmer and the SNA LAN product communications programmer.

The DB/2 CICS applications, the LAN-based application, and the communications subsystem can be developed and tested separately. The LAN application can view the CICS application as another input/output, and the CICS application can view the LAN application in the same manner.

The LU6.2 piece must be developed to accommodate the specifications for the input/output definitions for the two sides of the application. These specifications can be developed much like a client/server architecture, with the notable exception of an application/network bridge which the transactions traverse.

The gateway communications strategy is designed so that application programmers in either environment require no more knowledge than writing to the particular file designated as the mainframe application or LAN application. Using this strategy, teams may work independently, but the communications piece bears the responsibility for the integration.

This method provides an independent utilization of existing resources within an organization which has distributed the responsibility of the seven-layered OSI network architecture over as many departments.

10

An Example Network to Support Client/Server Applications

This chapter demonstrates the components of a network infrastructure (see Fig. 10.1) which allows users on a remote LAN running Netbios protocols to access data on a corporate LAN residing on Windows NT platforms running a Sequel database, data on a UNIX platform running an Oracle server, and data stored on a main-frame in VSAM and DB/2. The end result is a seamless interface from the client workstation to any of these back-end systems.

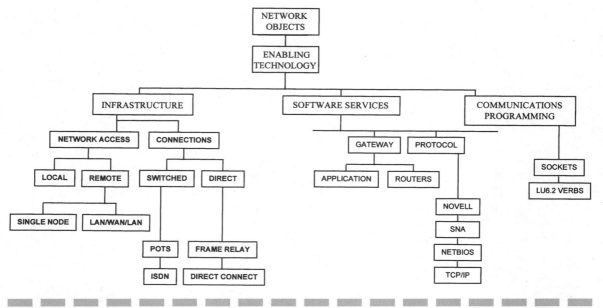

Figure 10.1 Example network components.

In this example, the remote LAN must be connected via a WAN protocol to a platform on the local corporate server; a backup is also required. Several candidates were available. These included frame relay, ISDN, and point-to-point direct leased line to extend the LAN networks. In this case, a frame relay primary with ISDN backup was selected. The biggest factor in this selection was cost. It was cheaper to pay for the frame relay line than to pay the tool charges for the ISDN connection. Should frame relay go down, ISDN is used to support the connection until frame relay is back on-line.

In addition to these LAN-to-LAN connections, back-end connectivity from the gateway LAN to the corporate SNA network had to be configured. In this case, a T1 existed between the gateway LAN and the token ring LAN supporting the mainframe. The other option here would be a point-to-point connection using the SDLC protocol between the actual gateway platform and the FEP 3745 supporting the mainframe link. Either way, this back end supports LU6.2, whereas the front-end client processes support TCP/IP. Figure 10.2 shows the resolution for this integration requirement.

Figure 10.3 is an application-to-application depiction of the architecture described above. It shows an application gateway on the remote Netbios node that accepts requests via Netbios and moves these requests

Figure 10.2
Overview of network integration.

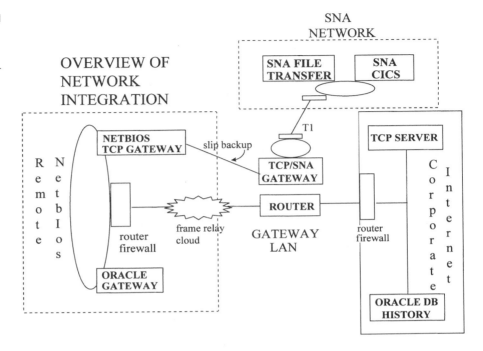

Figure 10.3
Application-to-application depiction of network integration.

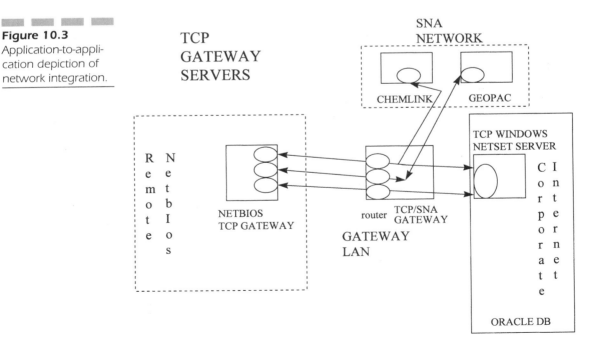

from Netbios to TCP/IP. The back end shows the gateway hosting three separate proxy services; one goes to the TCP Windows server, and the other two go to separate SNA systems. On the Netbios gateway are three client processes that request data from each of these proxy services depending on the client application requirements.

The next several illustrations are designed to show the configuration needed on the gateway to support both the TCP/IP connection and the back-end LU6.2 SNA connections to the mainframe. Beginning with the physical layer, Fig. 10.4 shows the three networks to which the gateway belongs: the SNA network, connected via the token ring card; the customer access network connected via frame relay and one of the Ethernet cards; and finally the corporate LAN, connected by the other Ethernet card. The gateway is configured with the TCP/IP stack running over the corporate LAN as well as the customer access network. The token ring card is configured with the SNA stack provided by the SNA service product from the RS6000 vendor. Other gateways, such as Sun's SUN-LINK peer-to-peer, provide the LU6.2 interface and the SNA stack.

Finally, the proxy services discussed above contain both socket interfaces to TCP/IP and LU6.2 interfaces to the SNA stack. Requests bound for SNA go through the sockets interface, and are sent out to the LU6.2 interface via the proxy program.

Figure 10,4
Gateway interface
cards.

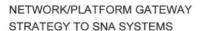
NETWORK/PLATFORM GATEWAY
STRATEGY TO SNA SYSTEMS

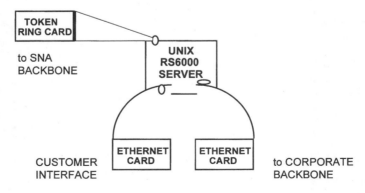

Gateway LAN

There are four phases to configuring an LU6.2 link: Phase 1 is the physical connection, phase 2 is the link connection, phase 3 is the session connectivity, and phase 4 is the conversation between the programs (proxy services on the gateway and a LU6.2 CICS transaction on the mainframe). This process is described below.

Figure 10.5 shows the configuration of the gateway and its relationship to the SNA backbone. It shows the token ring LAN to which the gateway is connected via the token ring card and the T1 extension from the local gateway to the remote LAN that actually hosts the mainframe 3745 with the network interface card (NIC).

Once this physical connection between the two LANs is set up, the Link-layer connections can operate (see Fig. 10.6). These are based on the addresses of the token ring cards. Most of the time, the original address of the card is not used for this purpose and a secondary address, assigned by the network administrator, is required. To establish this link layer, a VTAM GEN will have taken place which has among its parameters the token ring address of the NIC card in the gateway. Additionally, the VTAM GEN on the 3745 will contain an XID number. This number consists of IDBLK and the IDNUM. The IDBLK describes the type of platform. In addition, CPNAME will need to be configured on the gateway. The CPNAME is a combination of the mainframe node name and the ID of the network of which the target mainframe is a member.

Figure 10.5
Link connection.

NETWORK/PLATFORM GATEWAY STRATEGY

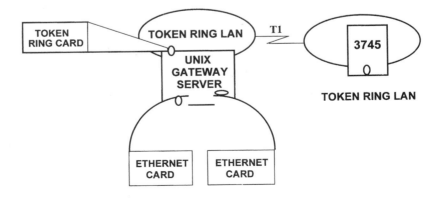

Figure 10.6
SNA link-layer parameters.

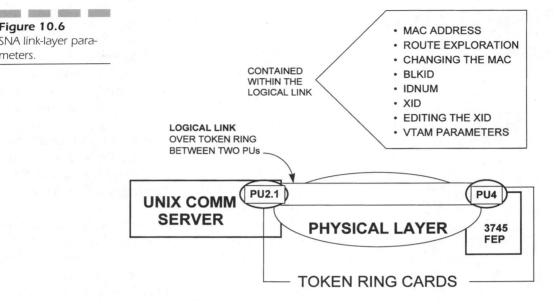

CONTAINED
WITHIN THE
LOGICAL LINK

- MAC ADDRESS
- ROUTE EXPLORATION
- CHANGING THE MAC
- BLKID
- IDNUM
- XID
- EDITING THE XID
- VTAM PARAMETERS

LOGICAL LINK
OVER TOKEN RING
BETWEEN TWO PUs

UNIX COMM SERVER PU2.1

PHYSICAL LAYER

PU4

3745
FEP

TOKEN RING CARDS

Once the link layer is set up and physical connections are in place, the next phase of the connection requires the establishment of session-layer connections between the UNIX communications gateway and the CICS application. This is accomplished through the connection of logical units (LUs) defined by VTAM. As Fig. 10.7 shows, the I55WCA00 has been defined as a logical unit name for the gateway. This logical unit is in session with another logical unit in the CICS region on the mainframe. At this point there are no conversations or application-to-application data exchanges occurring, but the logical and physical networking to support

Figure 10.7
Session-layer components.

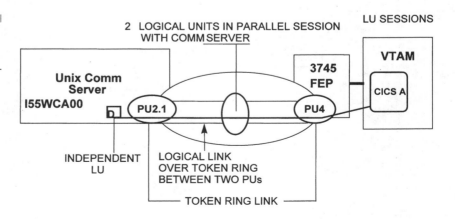

LU SESSIONS

2 LOGICAL UNITS IN PARALLEL SESSION
WITH COMM SERVER

VTAM

Unix Comm Server
I55WCA00

3745
FEP

CICS A

PU2.1

PU4

INDEPENDENT
LU

LOGICAL LINK
OVER TOKEN RING
BETWEEN TWO PUs

TOKEN RING LINK

conversations between programs are in place. A road between the gateway and the CICS application region has been built, over which conversation can now develop.

Figure 10.8 shows the addition of another CICS application over which logical sessions exist with the gateway. The LU names assigned to the CICS regions over which the sessions are in place are not shown. Multiple and parallel sessions can be supported between the gateway and some number of CICS regions. This enables the gateway to handle concurrent and multiple conversations with the CICS mainframe applications.

Figure 10.9 introduces the mode name parameter. The combination of the two LU names and the mode name identifies a unique session between two nodes over which applications can have conversations. For each of the three sessions shown, a unique combination of mode name, local LU (I55WCA00), and target LU is defined (CICS).

Figure 10.10 shows the program on the gateway using the SNA network connection to converse with a program running on the CICS mainframe. Chapters 14 & 15 explore the components of the SNA_TCP_Smo.c program to show how data is received from socket calls and then sent to SNA via LU6.2 interface verbs provided by the SNA server package running on the RS6000 or other gateway platform.

The next section shows how this same configuration is set up over SDLC links instead of token ring. Although the main differences are physical, the entire process is repeated so that the user may compare the differences and similarities.

Figure 10.8
Parallel sessions.

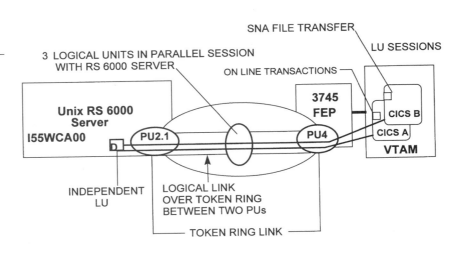

3 LOGICAL UNITS IN PARALLEL SESSION
WITH RS 6000 SERVER

SNA FILE TRANSFER

LU SESSIONS

ON LINE TRANSACTIONS

3745
FEP

Unix RS 6000
Server

I55WCA00

PU2.1

PU4

CICS B

CICS A

VTAM

INDEPENDENT
LU

LOGICAL LINK
OVER TOKEN RING
BETWEEN TWO PUs

TOKEN RING LINK

Figure 10.9
SNA conversations
over sessions.

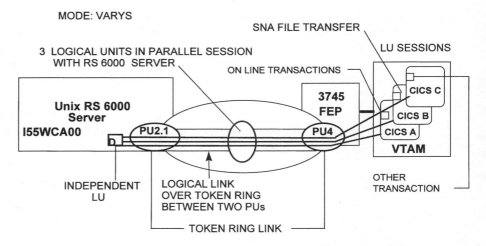

Figure 10.10
Program-to-program
conversation.

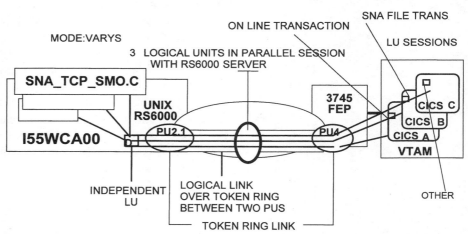

SNA Configuration

The LU6.2 protocol is primarily supported by two types of physical connections: point to point, or as a token ring station. The last section presented a token ring implementation; therefore, this section will focus on SDLC point-to-point.

Point-to-point lines are typically characterized by line speed; modem or null modem configurations; cable interfaces, such as RS-232, V.35, or 422; and clocking source. The speed requirements of the line dictate the type of cable interface, and the distance between the two platforms determines the need for two modems or a null modem configuration.

Since the mainframe does not provide clocking on the physical line (SNA architecture does not include a definition for physical connectivity), one of the modems or the other platform must provide it. Typically, the clocking is considered external and is provided by the modems.

Figure 10.11 depicts the physical connectivity from a Sun workstation to a mainframe through a front-end processor (FEP) running at 56 kbps.

The two platforms at which the line terminates for an LU6.2 connection usually will be a front-end processor, if connecting to a mainframe, and a personal computer or UNIX platform, if connecting to a LAN. If the line speed is over 19.2 kbps—and it is usually 56 kbps—the PC is usually configured with a separately purchased high-speed interface (HSI) board that supports a port to which the line from the modem will terminate. In the case of the Sun workstation, this can be an MCP board or an HSI board. These boards must be configured into the platform and properly addressed by the operating system. These boards typically support a high-speed cabling interface (Sun supports RS442; the interface supported by HP is proprietary). Because high-speed connections are supported in SNA by V.35 interfaces, a specially configured cable usually must be purchased to support this connection between the port on the platform and the modem or DSU.

The manuals which accompany the high-speed boards generally include instructions for testing whether the physical connection is working properly. This involves putting the remote DSU/modem in loopback mode, executing a program on the UNIX host to send packets out to the far-end modem, and then receiving those packets back from

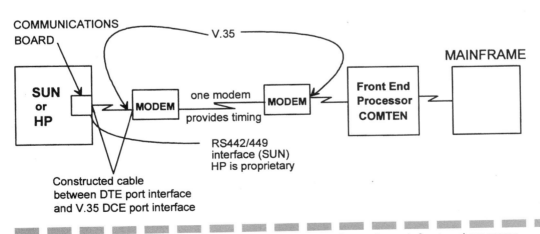

Figure 10.11 Physical connection of Sun workstation to mainframe through front-end processor.

the far-end modem. If all goes well, the physical loop is good, at least to the far-end modem. If the process fails—in other words, if the packets do not come back—then there is a problem on the physical line. This can include any of the following:

- Improperly configured modems, either speed setting or "clock setting"
- A bad cable between the modem and the port on the UNIX workstation
- A bad port on the board
- A bad high-speed board

Various tests can help determine the cause. For example, the local modem can be put in local loopback to test from the UNIX platform to the local modem. If this is OK and the far-end loopback is not, then the problem is between the two modems, or on the line. This would be a problem for the line provider.

However, if the packets fail to return from the local modem, a loopback plug can be used to test the connectivity from the UNIX platform to the port on the installed board and back again. If this fails, use the next check to help isolate the cause.

This last test checks for connectivity to the board. If any of these tests fail, the cause is probably a hardware problem internal to the Sun. If these internal checks to the port are OK, check the cable. Many times that is the cause of the problem. Also, double-check whether clocking is being supplied externally. This can also cause conflict. If clocking is off, usually some packets will be returned, but not all of them, and errors will appear on the line.

Once you are comfortable with the physical line, or if you just want to go ahead and configure the platform to the front-end processor on the SNA network, you must address the link-level parameters.

Link-Level Configuration

The link-level configuration requires the VTAM programmer to have completed a VTAM GEN which identifies and defines the UNIX box as a member of the SNA network. This includes definition of the physical unit (PU) address and type. In LU6.2 connections, there can be two types of PUs: 2.1 or 2.0.

A PU2.1 allows for independent LU6.2 nodes; a PU2.0 allows for LU6.2 sessions, but as dependent LUs. This nomenclature determines the network nodes' status and functionality in an SNA environment.

When PU2.0 nodes are being defined, there are few parameters which must be selected, since they will be negotiated and determined by VTAM. As stated, the VTAM definitions define a line and port on the FEP and configure it to the specific PU address and local LUs associated with that PU. These PU and LU resources are designated on the UNIX platform as a function of the purchased SNA gateway package.

The link-layer definition for a point-to-point connection to a physical unit type 2.0 on a UNIX platform with associated local LUs is shown in Fig. 10.12. The physical-layer definitions are repeated so that the relationship between the layers can be seen more clearly. Imagine that the link layer is just placed on top of the physical layer.

It is important to note that the PU address and the local LU names are all parameters provided by the VTAM programmer and defined to VTAM through the VTAM GEN.

At this point, the gateway software product on the UNIX platform can be started, and the link-layer connectivity tested.

Connectivity Test Results

If the gateway is started and the link-layer connectivity is not working, there are things you can check for:

- Verify the physical layer's integrity.
- Verify that the mainframe is polling the UNIX platform.

These things can be checked for by putting a "scope" on the line. The VTAM person working on the project should be able to assist you with this. The scope will tell you whether NCP is polling for responses from the newly defined PU. If it is, you can also check the PU address parameter, which may also be causing problems.

NCP will poll for a specific PU address, which is a number. If the PU address is not defined on the UNIX platform with the same number that is known to VTAM, this will cause the link not to activate. In addition, make sure that the PU type is defined as 2.0 and that it is a dependent PU. However, this is not as critical, since the physical unit will default to PU2.0 once the negotiation takes place. If there is no answer

[a] PHYSICAL LAYER

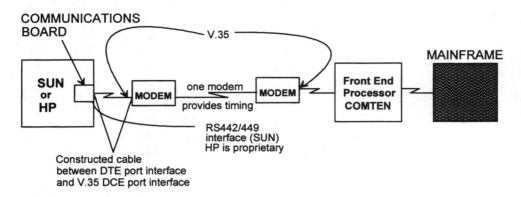

[b] LINK LAYER

Figure 10.12 (a) Physical-layer definitions. (b) Link-layer definitions.

back from the NCP polling and the physical line has been verified, the problem is probably the PU address.

Next, verify that the local LUs are active in VTAM. This means that the LUs are known to VTAM, and that when a session with one of them is requested, the routing tables in the mainframe know where they are. If there is a problem, check the numbers that have been assigned to the local LUs as well as the names, to be sure that they match those in the VTAM configuration. A mismatch can prevent the LUs from becoming active.

After some analysis and parameter adjustments, when the link is up and the local LUs are active in VTAM, you can test the session-level connectivity to the CICS application regions you need to talk to. However, if any changes are required, such as moving the UNIX platform, you may need to make additional checks. For example, if you need a new circuit, you need to verify the physical line again. You also need to check the link-level parameters.

It is important to remember that the physical port on the FEP expects to see only the PU address and LU names and addresses that have been assigned to it. This is particularly significant if you have to move the UNIX platform and need to connect another circuit to it. That new circuit must be plugged into the correct FEP port in order for it to work.

Session-Layer Connectivity

The session-layer connections are established between logical LUs. These LUs are associated with a PU as described above. Conversations between programs take place over the LUs. As noted in the link-layer discussion, the LUs are defined by the VTAM programmer along with the PU on the UNIX platform.

Once an LU is active, it is possible to try and establish a conversation with the partner LU. This partner LU is a known entity and represents the CICS application or other LU6.2 application you are trying to converse with. The CICS applications programmer who is writing the other transaction program which will run under the CICS mainframe region should give you the name of his or her LU, as well as the mode name, which represents a class of service for the LU sessions.

When all of these parameters have been correctly configured into the UNIX gateway, you can try to start a session. Sessions can come up in two ways:

- They can be started by the UNIX gateway, as in the case of HP using SNAPMANAGE.
- They can be initialized to come up when the gateway is started (Sun or HP).

A third alternative is to wait and let the conversation verb mc_allocate start the sessions for you, but this is more difficult to test.

However, if you are working with a CICS partner and want to demonstrate the connectivity to him or her, let the CICS program do an "acquire" on the session. This informs the CICS side that all is well, and if there is trouble with the session-layer connection, it can be diagnosed by looking in the CICS log.

Diagnosing Problems If the session does not acquire for some reason, there is trouble. Obvious problems to check for might be the following:

- There may be mismatched parameters such as local LUs, partner LU names, and mode name entries.

- More than one session may have been designated on a single-session dependent LU type.

- Your local LU may not be defined to CICS in the TERM table. You need to check with the CICS systems programmer to confirm this.

- Routing may not be correct in SNA. This is more difficult to detect and requires a VTAM programmer's assistance.

- The CICS programmer can look into the log and determine the reason for the failure. Or, you may be able to look into the SNA trace files on the UNIX platform. Look for a SENSE CODE = to determine the source of the problem.

- Finally, check whether the link is still active and the gateway is running.

Failure at any supporting level will cause the layer above to fail. Session problems are often caused by a failure in the levels below the session level. This is particularly true once the sessions are active and conversations are occurring.

Figure 10.13 displays the relationship between the local LUs and the underlying link and physical layers.

Many times the session level will appear to be OK, even though the link layer or physical layer has been disrupted for some reason. However, attempts to send data will fail when the conversation tries to use the dormant session.

In this event, it is necessary to restart the gateway at the link layer. Refer to Chap. 9, for information. Restarting the gateway should correct the problem. If it does not, and the partner system has restarted its resource as well, then there may be a problem on the physical line. The VTAM programmer should diagnose the problem.

Figure 10.13 also illustrates the use of multiple sessions over a given link, with the single sessions between each of the LU partners.

Note in this example that the CICS A and CICS C LUs, representing the CICS applications, are in fact holding multiple sessions. That is, one LU is having a session with more than one other LU. This is permitted in PU2.0 architecture. It is parallel sessions which require PU2.1 LEN sup-

[a] PHYSICAL LAYER

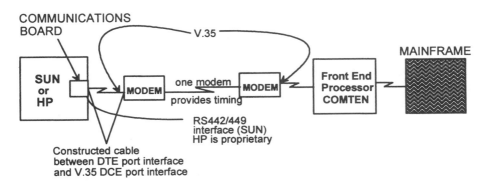

[b] LINK LAYER

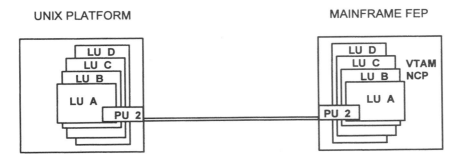

[c] ONE SESSION PER LU PAIR
MULTIPLE SESSION OVER A
GIVEN LINK

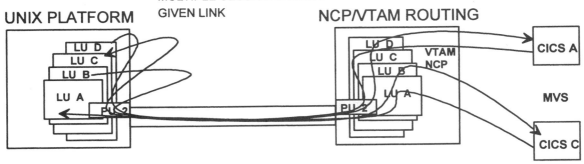

Figure 10.13 Relationship between local LUs and the underlying link and physical layers. (*a*) Physical layer. (*b*) Link-layer definitions. (*c*) One session per LU pair.

port. Parallel sessions are defined as two partner LUs having more than one session between themselves at the same time, thereby hosting many conversations.

Conversation Connectivity

With the successful configuration of the session-layer connections, link-layer connections, and physical-layer connections, testing of the conversation between the programs can begin. Refer to Chaps. 12 and 13 for a detailed example of LU6.2 programming.

11

Communications Programming

This chapter discusses in detail the basic concepts used in communications programming. Subjects include asynchronous vs. synchronous communications, peer-to-peer vs. client/server, sockets vs. APPC, and interprocess communications: message queues vs. socket calls (see Fig. 11.1).

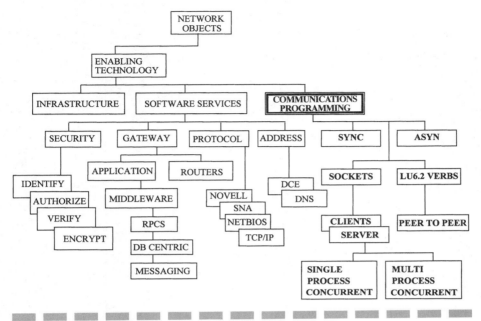

Figure 11.1 Basic communication programming concepts.

Asynchronous vs. Synchronous Communications

Communication programs are implemented as synchronous or asynchronous. Synchronous communications require a response from the partner before the communications subsystem returns to the application issuing the communications request. Therefore, all the processing done by the application waits until the response is returned.

Besides creating a long and unnecessary wait for the user on the client application, this type of implementation also wastes both platform and network resources with idle time. However, synchronous applications are useful in some instances, especially those which require immediate confirmation of an update.

Although asynchronous solutions that provide confirmation exist, they are more complicated to implement than a simple synchronous call. For example, sending a transaction from a Windows environment through an application gateway onto a mainframe database to effect an update can be done either synchronously or asynchronously, or a combination of the two. When it is done synchronously, a response comes back over the same programs and network conversation that initiated the transaction. When it is done asynchronously, the response to the transaction is handled over a different network resource and different conversation.

While the initiating program may not wait for the data, it still must poll for responses from the server handling the initial communications request. Between such peeks, the sending program is free to send additional transactions or do other work related to the application. In a synchronous mode, the program just waits for the response to be received. Nothing else happens until that occurs.

Peer-to-Peer vs. Client/Server

Well described in the literature, the difference between peer-to-peer and client/server programming lies in the ability of one program to start a conversation with the other. Client programs start conversations with servers and receive responses back. In a peer-to-peer model, either program may initiate the conversation. This difference is more pronounced in the synchronous model than in the asynchronous. However, this difference is overstated. In many instances client programs become server programs, and server programs often operate as client programs. This is particularly true for totally asynchronous solutions.

The main difference between peer-to-peer and client/server programming is the implications for the data stream received by the communications platform. Because peer-to-peer is implemented at the application layer, the client/server is often implemented using Berkeley sockets, the interface between the session-layer and the transport-layer data is processed in peer to peer as logical records, whereas in client/server on Berkeley sockets, data is sent and received as streams. A record has no meaning to programs operating at the socket layer. For this reason, many such implementations use Remote Procedure Calls (RPCs) for the session layer and allow communications interfaces to operate at the application layer. However, these solutions create synchronous-only communications.

Most of the complexity associated with LAN-to-mainframe implementation is attributable to the nature of the SNA LU6.2 programming paradigm, which has its origins in the PU2.0-dependent LU6.2 network architecture. But that does not have to be such a limiting factor today.

The use of parallel session technology by PU2.1 and independent LU6.2 architecture can simplify the connection of LAN workstations to mainframe data stores.

Unfortunately, the old PU2.0 model seems to have a firm hold on the mainframe establishment. Because the asynchronous model is a reasonable way to do business between SNA mainframes, the benefits and simplicity of the synchronous model for LAN clients running over TCP/IP and an SNA backbone are not well understood. This article attempts to highlight those benefits.

Using PU2.0 technology, a program opens a conversation on a session to a SNA host partner. The conversation then stays active to receive a continuous flow of messages from the partner to the host machine. Usually there are two conversations. Each conversation is one-way, with the possible exceptions of acknowledgments from the client. A separate program on the host then executes to return responses from the originating program.

In the synchronous model, using PU2.1 technology, a specific number of sessions are preallocated between the independent LUs. These sessions are then available to host parallel simultaneous conversations between different programs or instances of the same program. The conversation sends a message and waits for a reply on the same conversation. Once the reply is received, the conversation is deallocated, and another process may use the session for a different conversation. These are transaction-based processes. Multiple transactions between the two LUs are hosted via the multiple sessions and multiple conversations.

Between mainframes, the SNA asynchronous model has always been preferred. Whether this is also the case between gateway processes hosting TCP/IP socket servers that connect via LU6.2 is less clear.

Gateway Strategies

Before the development of PU2.1 nodes and independent LUs, TCP/IP gateways acted as multiplexers for SNA networks. Regardless of how many clients the TCP server hosted simultaneously, the requests were always bundled and sent to the host over one or several conversations which were always occupying the session. This model was typically applied to short requests coming in and long responses being received by the two partner programs. Also, it was the only way to do business from the SNA PU2.0 nodes.

Regardless of which client requested the data, the response was bunched up on one conversation and sent to the SNA system for processing. Meanwhile, if the conversation was synchronous, the TCP client waited for a response from the service. Once the response was returned from the mainframe, it was routed via header information to the requesting client.

With PU2.1 nodes, it is now possible for a TCP client to have synchronous conversations with a mainframe-based process via an LU6.2 conversation. Using a classic client/server model, the TCP sockets client sends a request to the mainframe and receives a response as if a subroutine call had been performed. And 255 of these calls may be handled simultaneously between two independent LUs.

This method of doing business can be considered when very high valued transactions are at stake, especially when long transactions are being sent and short replies are being received. It is useful because of the simplicity of the model and programming required to implement it.

There are similar methods of doing business between TCP clients and SNA servers that retain the asynchronous nature of mainframe programming but implement a synchronous conversation with the TCP clients, and simulate it with the SNA server. For example, the gateway may receive multiple requests from clients, fork a new process for each request, then open a conversation on the mainframe with the SNA service, send the request, receive a confirm deallocated, and cause the TCP client to wait on queue for a response. Once the response is received, the transaction is placed on the queue and returned by the waiting TCP client. This method is often used when short requests for data cause longer responses from the mainframe.

Sockets vs. APPC-LU6.2 Verbs

In both of these instances, APIs are used to request services from network resources. Generally, client programs are the ones which initiate a request, send the data for the request, and receive a response. Server programs generally listen for requests, receive the request, and return the response.

A server program using Berkeley sockets issues the following calls to get a network resource:

■ BIND. Advertises the service to the system so that all connection requests coming into the system get forwarded to this process.

- LISTEN. Listens for any connection requests on that bound address.
- ACCEPT. Accepts any connection requests heard from the LISTEN.
- FORK. Starts a new process to handle the client's request.
- READ. Reads the data from the request.
- WRITE. Writes the data to the client connection.
- CLOSE. Closes the connection to the client.

A client program using Berkeley sockets does a

- Socket to get an available resource.
- Connect to establish communications with the intended server at a PI address and port number.
- Send on the socket to move data from the client to the server.
- Receive on the socket to get response from the server.
- Close to shut down communications with the client.

With an LU6.2 peer-to-peer implementation:

- The client does an allocate to initiate a session with a destination LU (synonymous with IP address). The allocate starts a program running on the requested LU (similar to port number). The program then starts up and issues a receive and wait for data from the resource that requested it.
- The client program then sends the data with the send command and goes into receive and wait mode, waiting for a response. The receive and wait then returns to the LU6.2 server program.
- The server program fulfills the request and does a send to the client.
- The client, already in receive and wait mode, receives the response. At this point, the client may free the session with a deallocate or send another request.

Synchronous implementations of socket-based clients are similar. The socket, connect, send, and receive (or read and write issued on the socket) are handled via the Berkeley sockets implementation.

A network resource is returned from the socket call, a connect to service is returned via the connect, and the send on the socket connection returned from the connect waits until the data is received at the destination before returning. Likewise, a receive or read on the connection returns after data has been delivered from the platform to which the initial connection was made.

In LU6.2 implementations, a program is typically started with a connection to a server on a mainframe. This connection stays active while different user programs send and receive on the same conversation. Typically, there is one conversation between two processes or programs. In TCP/IP, there may be many simultaneous connections from multiple processes to one server.

On a Berkeley sockets connection, many different client connections come and go during the course of the day. On most LU6.2 implementations, a single conversation stays active for much longer periods of time.

The following illustrations help clarify how these programs work together.

Figure 11.2 shows the process listening on the socket and accepting a request (1); then it forks (2) to provide the write to message queue service (3a) and log the DB log (3b). The mainframe programs then access the message queue (4). The LU6.2 send program reads the message queue and writes to the mainframe (5). Meanwhile, the read from mainframe listens for responses (6) and writes them to the message queue (7).

Interprocess Communications

Given the one-to-many ratio between socket clients and server and the one-to-one ratio between peer processes, a multiplexing technique is generally employed to enable the many client programs to access the one conversation between the LU6.2 services. Interprocess communications (IPCs) are used on the server side. There are a number of implementations for UNIX and NT IPCs.

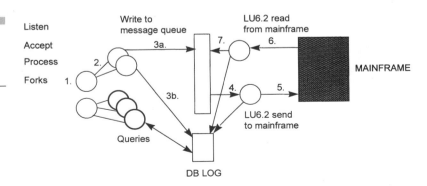

Figure 11.2
Concurrent multiple single-threaded processes.

The two most common are message queues and intraplatform sockets. Messages queues are reserved space in memory to which multiple programs write and from which a single program reads. In this case, there may be several client programs writing their requests for a service into a message queue. The service then reads the message queue and processes the requests. Multiple processes writing to a single queue and one process reading from it accomplish the multiplexing required.

The other method uses client/server techniques to implement an asynchronous connection between processes (see Fig. 11.3). In this case, multiple clients write to a service; the service then becomes a client to another service (perhaps a mainframe LU6.2 program), and writes the requests out to that service.

These implementations must be done asynchronously, so that the programs do not block, as programs of this type must continually check for incoming data, read it, and write it out. Blocking, if it occurs, is on the input side of these applications.

This implementation consideration is to balance the use of concurrent single multiplexed processes and message queues against the overhead and management of message queues.

Concurrent Single Multiplexed Sockets Server

The rest of this chapter presents a C++ wrapper implementation of a concurrent single multiplexed sockets server class and an LU6.2 verb class. These two classes are used by a TCP-to-SNA implementation.

There are good reasons for using C++ wrapper techniques to implement these sockets and SNA verb network calls. First, while data encapsulation can be designed into the C implementation, it is enforced in the

Figure 11.3
Concurrent single
multiplexed process.

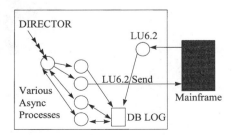

C++ classes. Second, the C classes can be used to create additional classes (derived classes) needed by other application programs. Other features of C++, such as polymorphism, where the same function names different arguments, are used in the cServer and cClient classes, which are derived from the cTCPnet base class. Figure 11.4 shows the object diagram depicting the classes used for this implementation. The cServer class and cSNAServer class are discussed in this chapter; Chap. 12 presents the base classes, and Chap. 13 presents a simple implementation using the cClient class defined below.

First, an implementation which uses two classes, cServer and cSNAServer, is presented. This application takes messages in via TCP/IP sockets, writes them out to an SNA LU6.2 network, waits for the response, then logs the message coming back.

This documentation will illustrate the use of a derived cServer TCP class to read the requests coming in and the use of a cSNAServer class to write the requests to the network. The application code is presented here and shows the objects being used. Along with the SNA and TCP server objects, the use of the cFDset class is needed to implement the single-process concurrent model. Though the cFDset class is not visible to the application TCPSNA.cpp, it is used by the cServer class and the cClient class to implement the asynchronous read and write and by the cServer class to implement the concurrent server model. These base classes are presented in Chap. 12.

The documentation below outlines the TCPSNA.cpp program shown in Fig. 11.5.

TCPSNA.cpp

```
#include <sys/types.h>
#include <sys/select.h>
#include <sys/socket.h>
```

Figure 11.4
Defined classes for
TCP/SNA client/server
communications.

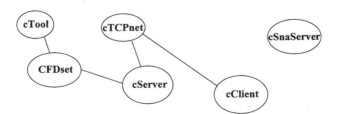

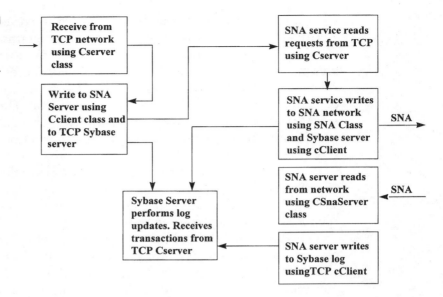

Figure 11.5
Applications using
TCP and SNA objects.

```c
#include <macros.h>
#include <stdio.h>
#include <stdlib.h>
#include <time.h>
#include <unistd.h>
#include <netinet/in.h>

#include <stdio.h>
#include <memory.h>
#include "cfdset.hpp"
#include "cserver.hpp"
#include "common.h"
#include "sna.h"

struct logInfo *mystructures;
#define QLEN    5
#define BUFSIZE4096

#define MAX_CONFIRMS   25

void
main (int argc, char *argv[])
{
cServer backend("backend", 1,5,"tcp");
cSNAserver sna(3200, "TITAN");

int msock, fd, nfds, sends = 0;

short amountReceived = 0;
int confirm = 0;
```

```
if(sna.connectRequestOutgoing()! = 0)
    errexit("Error allocating mainframe session\n ");
msock = backend.allocSocket();
    mystructures = (struct logInfo *) memcheck(malloc(nfds *
sizeof(*mystructures)));
        while(1)
        {
    int ssock;
        ssock = backend.cServerProtReady(msock);
        if(ssock < 0 )
            errexit("accpt: %s\n", sys_errlist[errno]);


        mystructure = backend.cReceive(&ssock);

            if(sna.send(mystructures[fd].message, !(++sends %
MAX_CONFIRMS)))
            {
            printf("Unable to send\n");
            }
            else if(sna.receive(mystructures[fd].message,
                amountReceived, confirm))
            {
            printf("Unable to receive\n");
            }
            else
            printf("Received from Mainframe successfully = >%s< = \n",
                mystructures[fd].message);
            memset(&mystructures[fd], 0, sizeof mystructures[fd]);
            }


            }

            if(sna.disconnect() = = 0)
            {
            printf("SNA Disconnect Issued\n");
        }
    }
```

This program illustrates the simplicity of a complicated application gateway program which reads from the TCP network and writes to the SNA network, then waits for a response and reads from the SNA network. With the use of two classes, cServer and cSNAServer, the complexity of the network protocols is transparent to the application. The sna.connectRequestOutgoing() handles the initial setup and contact with the SNA partner program. And the backend.allocSocket() program starts the program as a TCP sockets program and establishes this program as a service on the TCP network.

The program basically runs forever, checking for connection requests via the backend.cServerProtReady() function and then reading those messages via the backend.cReceive() function. Once a message is received, the program passes the message to the sna.send object, which sends it to the SNA network. The sna.receive is called next to wait for a response from the SNA program receiving the message above. Once received, the message is displayed on the screen.

Presented below is the cServer.cpp class.

cServer.hpp

```
#ifndef__CSERVER_H
#define__CSERVER_H
#include <sys/types.h>
#include <sys/socket.h>
#include <netinet/in.h>
#include "errexit.hpp"
#include "ctcpnet.hpp"
#include "cfdset.hpp"
#include "ctool.hpp"
/*****************************************************/
/*          Name: cServer.hpp                        */
/*****************************************************/
struct serv  {
            //1char    service[10];
            char       servN[10];
            char       rcv_buf[4096];
            };
struct serv table[5];
class cTool;
class cServer: public cTCPnet {
private:
    cFDset afds,rfds,wfds;
    cTool ctool;
    int     services_no, qLen;
    int     type, nfds, count ;
    char    protocol[64];
    char    bufRead[4096];
    int     sockDesc, size, statFlag, bufSize, msocket;
    char    servName[64];
    //fd_set  *pafds;
    struct sockaddr_in serverAddr, myAddr, targetAddr;
    struct sockaddr_in clientAddr;
    char    *buf;
    char    *host;
    struct sockaddr_in fsin;
public:
    cServer( char*     serviceName,
         int  flag, int qlen = 5, char *protocol = "tcp");
    ~cServer(void){}
    int allocSocket();
        int cServerProtReady(int);
    int cAccept(void);
    char *cReceive (int*);
        void sendTCP(char *buf, int buf_len, int);
};

#endif//__CSERVER_H
```

cServer.cpp

```cpp
#include <sys/param.h>
#include <sys/types.h>
#include <sys/select.h>
#include <sys/socket.h>
#include <sys/ioctl.h>
#include <strings.h>
#include <stdio.h>
#include <netdb.h>
#include <stdlib.h>
#include <stddef.h>
#include <unistd.h>
#include <netinet/in.h>
#include <arpa/inet.h>
#include "ctool.hpp"
#include <iostream.h>
//#include "common.h"
#include "cserver.hpp"

//struct services table[5];

//class cFDset;
const int portbase = 0;
extern int errno;
extern char *sys_errlist[];

cServer::cServer(char* serviceName, int flag, int qlen, char
*proto)
{

        strcpy(servName, serviceName);
        statFlag = flag;
        strcpy(protocol, proto);
        qLen = qlen;
          afds.FDzero();
};
```

This constructor function sets the variables used by the instance of the class. Included is the serviceName, which is later used by allocSocket to find the port number on which the service is running as defined in the /etc/services file. Next, the qlen variable sets the length of the request queue for the service before requests to connect are rejected. Finally, the proto variable defines the protocol; in most instances this will be TCP as opposed to UDP. The afds.FDzero function is a member of the cFDset class and is used to set the variable afds to zero. Afds is defined in the cFDset class and is used to hold indicators used by the select call, which determine whether a particular port is ready for input or output. The select call, along with the functions described in cFDset, allows the server to service multiple client requests as explained below.

```
int cServer::allocSocket()
{
    struct servent *pse; /* pointer to service information entry*/
    struct protoent *ppe; /*pointer to protocol information entry
    */
    struct sockaddr_in sin; /* internet endpoint */
    int s, type; /* socket descriptor and type */

    bzero ((char *)&sin, sizeof (sin));
    sin.sin_family = AF_INET;
    sin.sin_addr.s_addr = INADDR_ANY;

/* map service name to port number */
    cout <<"calling getservbyname"<<endl;

        if (pse = getservbyname(servName,"tcp"))
            sin.sin_port = htons(ntohs((u_short)pse->s_port) + port-
            base);

        else if ( ( sin.sin_port = htons ((u_short) atoi(servName)))
        = = 0)
        errexit ( "cant get \"%s\" protocol entry\n", servName);

        type = SOCK_STREAM;
/* allocate a socket */
    cout <<"calling socket" <<endl;

        sockDesc = socket(PF_INET, type, 0);
        if(sockDesc < 0)
        errexit("cant create socket : %s\n", sys_errlist[errno]);

        /* bind the socket */

    cout << "calling bind" << endl ;
        if(bind (sockDesc, (struct sockaddr *)&sin, sizeof (sin))
        <0)
        errexit ("cant bind to %s port: %s\n", servName,
        sys_errlist[errno]);

    cout << "calling listen" << endl;

        if (type = = SOCK_STREAM && listen(sockDesc,qLen) < 0)
        errexit("cant listen on %s port: %s\n", servName,
            sys_errlist[errno]);
        cout << "listening on socket"<< sockDesc << endl;
        afds.FDset(sockDesc);
        nfds = getdtablesize();
        return sockDesc;


}
```

There are seven functions combined in the allocSocket function to set up the service on the platform. These seven functions are

1. *getservbyname*(*servName*, *"tcp"*). This function is used to read the /etc/services file and look up the port address reserved for this particular service on the host machine. When the client attempts to connect to this service, it will use this port number to locate the service on the target platform.

2. *sin.sin_port = **htons ((u_short) atoi(servName)))**.* This function is used to translate the port number returned by getservbyname into a port address that can be advertised as the address on which this service is listening.

3. *sockDesc = **socket**(PF_INET, type, 0);.* This function returns the socket number associated with the port on which the service will listen for connections and accept requests. This is an internal number and is not related to the port number in the sense that the socket can be different for each invocation of the service and need not be known to the client. The port number, on the other hand, is a value shared by the service and the client wishing to use the service. The PF_INET variable tells the socket function that it will be valid for connection requests coming in for any IP address valid for the listening platform. In cases where a platform may have multiple IP addresses assigned to it, requests arriving on any of these IP addresses are processed by this service.

4. *(**bind** (sockDesc, (struct sockaddr*)&sin, sizeof (sin)) <0).* The bind function combines any net IP address, the port number, the protocol, and the socket descriptor with the server process so that the address of the server becomes this combination.

5. *listen(sockDesc,qLen).* Based on the combined address from the bind, the listen function waits for connections on it. This function blocks until a request is received.

6. *afds.**FDset**(sockDesc);.* This function is used to set the bit in the afds matrix that states the value found in the sockDesc and is available as the listener socket for this port. It is later used by the select call in the cServerProtReady function to detect a client wanting to make a connection on this particular service.

7. *= **getdtablesize()**;.* This function defines the maximum number of file entries or connections that can be available.

The returned value for sockDesc is the file descriptor integer value on which the server is listening for connections. It is passed to the routine below by the application program and used by that function.

```
int cServer::cServerProtReady(int socktest)
{
    int rdyfds;
    cout << "checking port ready accept/select call on port"
    <<socktest
<<endl;

        bcopy ( afds, rfds, sizeof(rfds));
    rdyfds = select(nfds, rfds, (fd_set *)0, (fd_set *)0, (struct
        timeval *)0);
```

```
     if (rdyfds <0)
         return ( rdyfds );
// errexit("select: %s\n", sys_errlist[errno]);

    cout <<" returning from accept/select call" << endl ;
    cout << "descriptors ready = "<< rdyfds << endl;
{
    if(rfds.isFDready(socktest))
        {
        int ssock;

  cout << "fd socket listen is ready to accept connection"
          << endl;

        ssock = cAccept();
        cout << "returning from accept connection on socket"
               << ssock << endl

        if(ssock < 0)
            errexit ("accpt: %s\n", sys_errlist[errno]);

    cout << "accept on socket" << ssock << endl;
    afds.FDset(ssock);
    return ssock;
    }
    cout <<"not ready on accept"<< endl ;
    return 0;
    }

};
```

The select call in this routine now blocks until a connection is requested on the port number returned by the listen () function. If a connection is present but no new connection is detected, the previous connection is used. If rfds.isFDready(socktest) is true, then the cAccept() call is used and the new connection is returned through ssock. This new connection returned by the cAccept() call is used to read the data in the cReceive call, which is described below.

```
int cServer::cAccept(void)
    {
        int rc;
        int alen;

        alen = sizeof(clientAddr);
        rc = accept(sockDesc, (struct sockaddr *)&clientAddr,
                     &alen);

        if (rc < 0)
            errexit(" Error in accepting\n");

        return rc;

    };
char* cServer::cReceive(int *active_conn)
{
char client_ip[80];
```

```
struct sockaddr_in  cli_addr;
        int fd, buf_len,cilen, client_port,gpn;
        char message_size[5];
        bcopy (afds, rfds, sizeof(rfds));
          cout << "calling select/receive" << endl;
              fd = *active_conn;
            clilen = sizeof(cli_addr);
gpn = getpeername(fd, (struct sockaddr *) & cli_addr,&clilen);
        if (gpn < 0) {
              printf ("get peername failed %d\n",gpn );
              }
            else
              {
sprintf(client_ip,"client addr = %s\n",
inet_ntoa(cli_addr.sin_addr)):
cout <<"clip = "<< client_ip<< "clport = "<<ntohs(
cli_addr.sin_port)<<"fd = "<<fd<<endl;
              }
        if (select(nfds, rfds, (fd_set *) 0, (fd_set *)0,(struct
        timeval *) 0) < 0)
                    errexit ("select failed\n");
        cout << "returning from select/receive" << endl ;
        for ( fd = 0: fd < nfds; ++fd) ){
            if(fd != sockDesc && rfds.isFDready(fd)){
                int byRead;
                  cout <<"read ready fd = " <<fd<<endl;
                  long now;
                  byRead = read(fd, message_size,4);
                  buf_len = atoi(message_size);
                  cout <<"buflen = "<<buf_len;
                  delete [] buf;
                  buf = new char[buf_len + 1];
                  byRead = read(fd, buf, buf_len);
                  if (byRead < 0)
                      errexit("error in reading \n");
                  if (buf_len = = 0){
                      afds.FDclear (fd );
                      close (fd);
                  }
                  (void) ctool.mstime(&now);
                  printf ("time = %d\n",now);
                  *active_conn = fd;
                  cout <<"active conn return =
                          "<<active_conn << endl ;
                  buf[buf_len] = NULL;
                  return buf;
            }
        }
    }
```

- The getpeername() is used to return the address (IP number and port number) of the sending client.

- The inet_ntoa() is used to translate the address into the decimal dot format that is printed.

- The ntohs() translates the port number to a string.

- This select() function checks to see if data has arrived on the port to which the connection has been received. This function blocks until data arrives on that port.

- The read function reads the message_size, which is contained within the first 4 bytes of each application message.

- The second read statement then reads the message, using the message length returned by the first read.

- Finally, the read port is cleared if there is no more data to read from the port number. With afds.FDclear(fd), the connection from the server to the port is closed. If there is only one connect, the server will now wait on a new connection at the accept call in the ServerPortReady() function.

The sendTCP() function discussed below is used to return data to the client from which the request was received.

It is also used to send a message to the client connected on the active_con connection. In this example, that connection is the connection on which the receive data was just issued. But it could really be any active connection which was waiting for a response from the server. In the application qserver, it is between the read and the write back to the client that the actual service is performed for the client.

```
void cServer::sendTCP(char* buf,int buf_len,int active_conn)
{
     char rec_len[] = "0000";
     int fd, i;
if(buf_len = = 0) {
   for (i = 0); i< 80; ++i)
        buf[i] = 'D';
}
   bcopy(afds, wfds, sizeof(wfds));
   (void ) ctool.mstime ((long *)0);/* set the epoch */
if (select(nfds, (fd_set *)0, wfds, (fd_set *)0,
         (struct timeval *)0)<0)
         return;
//         errexit("Select failed\n");
   cout <<" sendTCP" << endl;

       cout <<"activeconn = "<<active_conn<<"nfds = "<<nfds<<endl;

         for (fd = active_conn; fd < nfds; ++fd){
          printf ("fd = %d, nfds = %d\n",fd, nfds);
            printf ("looking for write fd = %d\n",fd);

              if(fd != sockDesc && wfds.isFDready(fd))
              {
              int cc;
              printf ("write fd = %d\n",fd);
              printf ("write = %s\n", buf);
```

```
                    sprintf (rec_len,"%4.4d",buf_len);
                    cc = write (fd,rec_len,4);
                    cc = write(fd,buf,buf_len);
//                     afds.FDclear(fd);
                    if ( cc < 0)
                            errexit("error in write\n");

        printf ("returning to mainfrom sendtcp\n");
        return ;
                    }
             }
        }
```

12

The LU6.2 Conversation Class

This chapter discusses the LU6.2 class used by programs to connect to the mainframe (see Fig. 12.1). First, an overview of LU6.2 programming is presented, along with an illustration of the networking needed to support the programs. Next, the class is presented, along with a detailed description of each of the subroutines and the verbs included in them.

Figure 12.1
LU6.2 conversation
class.

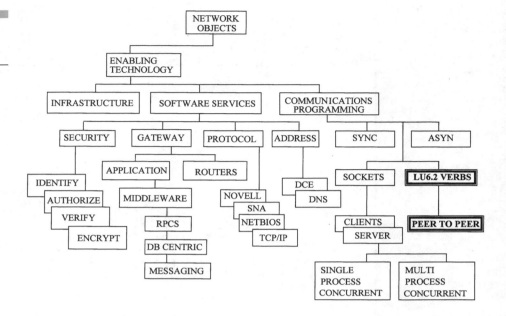

LU6.2 Conversation Background

The two conversation programs discussed in this chapter are written so that either one conversation is in send state and the other is in receive state, or a state change is anticipated.

Conversations are written as either synchronous or asynchronous. Conversations that are synchronous request that the partner TP confirm what the originating TP sent. For example, a conversation which sends data may request the receiving TP to confirm receipt of that information.

LU6.2 Verbs

Conversations make use of architected LU6.2 verbs. There are about 21 verbs, most of which you will not use. The primary list is made up of two types of verbs: session control verbs and conversation verbs.

Conversation verbs may be mapped or unmapped. Unmapped conversation verbs require the use of assembler language programs on the CICS region. The primary difference is that unmapped receives the generalized data stream. In the mapped conversation, a record written by the sending partner is a record read by the receiving partner.

Conversations can also be synchronous or asynchronous, mapped or unmapped.

Conversation Initiation

Conversations are designed to be started by one partner and received by the other. The starting partner issues an allocate verb with the name of the partner program to start on the receiving side. When the SNA LU6.2 stack receives the request to start the program, it loads the receiving program in memory, and execution begins. Figure 12.2 illustrates the protocol.

Depending on a number of start-up circumstances, the started TP receives the conversation request and goes into a receive and wait state, and waits for additional information from the requesting program. A positive acknowledgment (zero return code) is returned to the calling program if the LU6.2 allocate verb is successful.

If the allocate verb fails, a nonzero return code is returned. Failure is usually a result of one of two circumstances: inability to find the program requested or lack of permission to request that the program be run. These circumstances are usually distinguished by a message such as Resource not available or Resource not found. In this case, check to ensure the following:

- The proper names have been coded for the parameters for the allocate verb.
- CICS is giving you permission to execute the program.

Once the zero return code has been received on the allocate verb, a send verb can be issued with the data. Once the send has been issued, the partner should automatically detect it from the receive and wait verb and return the data to the program that issued the receive and wait verb.

This loop can continue until there is no more data to be sent to the receiver. Once it is complete, however, the sender must signal the receiver that all the data has been sent and the conversation is going to end (this is the typical scenario, but not the only one). This is done with the deallocate verb.

Once the deallocate verb is issued, the receiving partner follows its normal procedure, usually exiting, when it returns from the receive in the deallocated state.

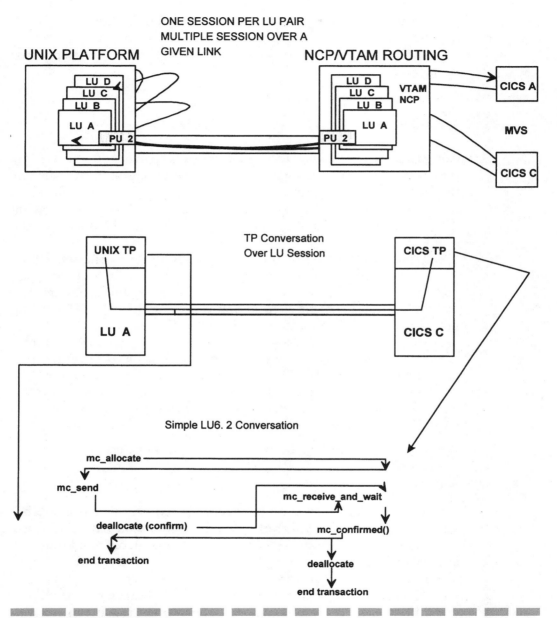

Figure 12.2 Example LU6.2 verb protocol.

The two verbs, send and deallocate, most commonly take advantage of the synchronous protocol, or the confirm verb. However, use of this feature can cause problems.

For example, coding a send and requesting a confirm from the partner program causes the sending program to wait for the confirm response from the target. If the target program does not recognize the confirm request and does not issue the confirm, the sending program hangs waiting for the confirm response, and the receiving program remains in a receive and wait state.

No errors will have occurred; however, the conversation will in effect be hung. This can be difficult to diagnose, and points up the need to keep things as simple as possible without sacrificing data integrity.

Other anomalies in LU6.2 conversation arise from the way data is sent, or is not sent, across the network. To provide efficient use of networking facilities, data is not necessarily sent at the time the send verb is issued, nor is the allocate necessarily requested at the time it is issued. The data is written to the buffer and is not sent to the partner program until the buffer fills, a flush() verb is issued, or the conversation changes state.

As a result, an error from a previously issued verb may not occur until the data is flushed onto the network and into the next program. This can give the illusion that a verb is working properly, since the error may not occur at the time the verb is issued.

Finally, the cSNAServer class is introduced. This provides object reference to the c functions provided in the RS6000 SNA server.

There are five major user interface functions coded into this class. The user uses them as appropriate. As previously discussed, a sending partner and receiving partner are coded to perform peer-to-peer processing. Usually one partner requests a session with the other, and the other receives the request as incoming. Two mutually exclusive functions to accomplish these two incoming and outgoing requests are available to the programmer.

The partner program initiating the request uses the connectRequestOutgoing, and the partner program receiving the request issues the connectRequestIncoming(). Once the function returns to the caller, the initiator usually issues the send() function and the receiver issues the receive() function. Coded within each of these public functions are LU6.2 CPIC verbs to implement these generic functions (see Fig. 12.3). The following are discussed below.

- cSNAserver::cSNAserver(int length, char *profileName, int sync)

- int cSNAserver::connectRequestIncoming()

Figure 12.3
Defined classes for
TCP/IP SNA
client/server commu-
nications.

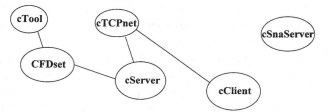

- int cSNAserver::connectRequestOutgoing(void)
- int cSNAserver::receive(char *in_data, short &received, int &confirm_requested)
- int cSNAserver::send (char *out_data, int confirm_command)

CSNASERVER.CPP

```cpp
#include <stdio.h>
#include <sys/types.h>
#include <fcntl.h>
#include <string.h>
#include <errno.h>
#include <stdlib.h>
#include <assert.h>
#include "sna.h"

/*─────────────────────────────────────────────────────────
 * ASCII to EBCDIC translation table.
 * This contains only the U.S. English character set, which is
 * known as the UGL (universal glyph list) character set.
 *─────────────────────────────────────────────────────────*/
const unsigned char ascii_to_ebcdic_table[] = {
/* 00-0F */
"\x00\x01\x02\x03\x37\x2D\x2E\x2F\x16\x05\x15\x0B\x0C\x0D\x0E\x0F"
/* 10-1F */
"\x10\x11\x12\x13\x3C\x3D\x32\x26\x18\x19\x3F\x27\x22\x1D\x35\x1F"
/* 20-2F */
"\x40\x5A\x7F\x7B\x5B\x6C\x50\x7D\x4D\x5D\x5C\x4E\x6B\x60\x4B\x61"
/* 30-3F */
"\xF0\xF1\xF2\xF3\xF4\xF5\xF6\xF7\xF8\xF9\x7A\x5E\x4C\x7E\x6E\x6F"
/* 40-4F */
"\x7C\xC1\xC2\xC3\xC4\xC5\xC6\xC7\xC8\xC9\xD1\xD2\xD3\xD4\xD5\xD6"
/* 50-5F */
"\xD7\xD8\xD9\xE2\xE3\xE4\xE5\xE6\xE7\xE8\xE9\xAD\xE0\xBD\x5F\x6D"
/* 60-6F */
"\x79\x81\x82\x83\x84\x85\x86\x87\x88\x89\x91\x92\x93\x94\x95\x96"
/* 70-7F */
"\x97\x98\x99\xA2\xA3\xA4\xA5\xA6\xA7\xA8\xA9\xC0\x4F\xD0\xA1\x07"
/* 80-8F */
"\x43\x20\x21\x1C\x23\xEB\x24\x9B\x71\x28\x38\x49\x90\xBA\xEC\xDF"
/* 90-9F */
```

```
"\x45\x29\x2A\x9D\x72\x2B\x8A\x9A\x67\x56\x64\x4A\x53\x68\x59\x46"
/* A0-AF */
"\xEA\xDA\x2C\xDE\x8B\x55\x41\xFE\x58\x51\x52\x48\x69\xDB\x8E\x8D"
/* B0-BF */
"\x73\x74\x75\xFA\x15\xB0\xB1\xB3\xB4\xB5\x6A\xB7\xB8\xB9\xCC\xBC"
/* C0-CF */
"\xAB\x3E\x3B\x0A\xBF\x8F\x3A\x14\xA0\x17\xCB\xCA\x1A\x1B\x9C\x04"
/* D0-DF */
"\x34\xEF\x1E\x06\x08\x09\x77\x70\xBE\xBB\xAC\x54\x63\x65\x66\x62"
/* E0-EF */
"\x30\x42\x47\x57\xEE\x33\xB6\xE1\xCD\xED\x36\x44\xCE\xCF\x31\xAA"
/* F0-FF */
"\xFC\x9E\xAE\x8C\xDD\xDC\x39\xFB\x80\xAF\xFD\x78\x76\xB2\x9F\xFF"
};

/*---------------------------------------------------------------
 * EBCDIC to ASCII translation table.
 * This contains only the U.S. English character set, which is
 * known as the UGL (universay glyph list) character set.
 *------------------------------------------------------------*/
const unsigned char ebcdic_to_ascii_table[] = {
/*00-0F */
"\x00\x01\x02\x03\xCF\x09\xD3\x7F\xD4\xD5\xC3\x0B\x0C\x0D\x0E\x0F"
/* 10-1F */
"\x10\x11\x12\x13\xC7\x0A\x08\xC9\x18\x19\xCC\xCD\x83\x1D\xD2\x1F"
/* 20-2F */
"\x81\x82\x1C\x84\x86\x0A\x17\x1B\x89\x91\x92\x95\xA2\x05\x06\x07"
/* 30-3F */
"\xE0\xEE\x16\xE5\xD0\x1E\xEA\x04\x8A\xF6\xC6\xC2\x14\x15\xC1\x1A"
/* 40-4F */
"\x20\xA6\xE1\x80\xEB\x90\x9F\xE2\xAB\x8B\x9B\x2E\x3C\x28\x2B\x7C"
/* 50-5F */
"\x26\xA9\xAA\x9C\xDB\xA5\x99\xE3\xA8\x9E\x21\x24\x2A\x29\x3B\x5E"
/* 60-6F */
"\x2D\x2F\xDF\xDC\x9A\xDD\xDE\x98\x9D\xAC\xBA\x2C\x25\x5F\x3E\x3F"
/* 70-7F */
"\xD7\x88\x94\xB0\xB1\xB2\xFC\xD6\xFB\x60\x3A\x23\x40\x27\x3D\x22"
/* 80-8F */
"\xF8\x61\x62\x63\x64\x65\x66\x67\x68\x69\x96\xA4\xF3\xAF\xAE\xC5"
/* 90-9F */
"\x8C\x6A\x6B\x6C\x6D\x6E\x6F\x70\x71\x72\x97\x87\xCE\x93\xF1\xFE"
/* A0-AF */
"\xC8\x7E\x73\x74\x75\x76\x77\x78\x79\x7A\xEF\xC0\xDA\x5B\xF2\xF9"
/* B0-BF */
"\xB5\xB6\xFD\xB7\xB8\xB9\xE6\xBB\xBC\xBD\x8D\xD9\xBF\x5D\xD8\xC4"
/* C0-CF */
"\x7B\x41\x42\x43\x44\x45\x46\x47\x48\x49\xCB\xCA\xBE\xE8\xEC\xED"
/* D0-DF */
"\x7D\x4A\x4B\x4C\x4D\x4E\x4F\x50\x51\x52\xA1\xAD\xF5\xF4\xA3\x8F"
/* E0-EF */
"\x5C\xE7\x53\x54\x55\x56\x57\x58\x59\x5A\xA0\x85\x8E\xE9\xE4\xD1"
/* F0-FF */
"\x30\x31\x32\x33\x34\x35\x36\x37\x38\x39\xB3\xF7\xF0\xFA\xA7\xFF"
};

#define OK        0
#define SEND_IND  0x005
cSNAserver::cSNAserver(int length, char*profileName, int sync)
{
```

```
allowed_length = length;
sprintf((char *)MainFrameProfileName, "%-8.8s", profileName);
sync_level = sync;
}
```

This constructor function, called by all the programs when the class object type is defined into the application, receives a *length* value which sets the maximum size record that the receive function can accept from the partner, and a *profile name* which references the network definitions for the LUs and mode name required by the connectRequestOutgoing function. This file names the local LU, the remote LU, and the mode name for the session. This session will eventually carry the conversation started by the connectRequestOutgoing. And this profile name argument describes that session to this CPIC function.

In addition to the session information, this profile contains the name of the remote transaction that is to be started on the remote system by the connectRequestOutgoing verb. This was described in Chap. 11.

The *sync* parameter is used to describe the nature of the conversation this program can have. Sync level 1 is common. Sync level 1 enables a conversation to accept confirm requests from the partner. A sync level 0 does not allow confirms, and a sync level 2 will request that transaction-level synchronization occur between two partners. Sync level 2 is usually not supported between different platforms and operating systems. It is rarely used where it is supported because of the overhead associated with this degree of synchronization.

```
int cSNAserver::connectRequestOutgoing(void)
    {
    CM_RETURN_CODE rtn_code;
    cminit (resource, MainFrameProfileName, &rtn_code);
    if (rtn_code != OK ) {
       printf("error from cminit = %d\n", rtn_code);
       return(rtn_code);
       }
       cmssl(resource, &sync_level, &rtn_code);
       if (rtn_code != OK )
          {
          printf("error from get activation info = %d\n",
               rtn_code);
          return(rtn_code);
          }
          cmallc (resource, &rtn_code);
          if(rtn_code != 0 )
            printf("error from m_allocate %d\n", rtn_code);
            return(rtn_code);

    } /* SNA_connect_request_outgoing */
```

This routine is called to establish a conversation over the session described by the profile name. This particular implementation is on the RS6000, but the information described in that profile must be provided in some form to this verb. The **cminit** and **cmssl** verbs set up the format for the **cmallc** call, which actually establishes the conversation with the other side. This verb is not actually sent over the network until a send () is sent along with a confirm(). This is an important consideration when doing program debugging.

```
/*******************************************************************/
/* This routine is called when the program being written is to
receive allocates as opposed to requesting an allocate
*/
/*******************************************************************/
int cSNAserver::connectRequestIncoming()
{
   CM_RETURN_CODE rtn_code;
   cmaccp (resource, &rtn_code);
   if(rtn_code != OK )
      {
      printf ("error from get activation info = %d\n", rtn_code);
      return(rtn_code);
      }
      return(rtn_code);
} /* SNA_connect_request_incoming */
```

This function is used by the receiving partner. It accepts the incoming request generated by the cmallc call above. The resource pointer referenced as a parameter is used by the send and receive calls for all subsequent conversation between the two partners.

```
int cSNAserver::send (char *out_data, int confirm_command)
{
   CM_REQUEST_TO_SEND_RECEIVED rq_to_send_rcvd;
   CM_RETURN_CODE rtn_code;
   long length = strlen(out_data);
   convert_ascii_to_ebcdic_field((unsigned char *) out_data, (int)
            length);
   cmsend (resource, (unsigned char *) out_data, &length,
            &rq_to_send_rcvd,
            &rtn_code);
   if(rtn_code != OK)
      {
      printf ("error from send_data %d\n" , rtn_code);
      return(rtn_code);
      }
      if(confirm_command == 1)
      cmcfm(resource,&rq_to_send_rcvd,&rtn_code);
      return(rtn_code);
} /* SNA_send_request */
```

When the program partner is the initiating one, the next thing that is done after the malloc is a send. The send verb moves user data from the originating program to the other partner across the network. If the two platforms share the same character set, EBCDIC or ASCII, there is no need for any translation of the data. If one is different, such as the mainframe being EBCDIC and all UNIX machines and PCs being ASCII, then a translation must occur if the data is to be read by the receiving partner. In the case above, the data is being sent from an ASCII machine (RS6000) to a mainframe, so a translation must occur. The convert_ascii-to-ebcdic_field function along with the tables defined in front of this class provide the translation. The address of the data is sent, translated, and returned to the function using the originating string.

The data is now ready to be sent to the partner machine. The cmsend command does this. If a confirm is requested by the application, then the cmcfm command is issued. This command immediately sends any buffered data from the originating platform across the network to the receiving partner.

If this is the first time, it is here that errors from previous verbs show up, as they are not actually sent over the network until the send command is issued.

```
int cSNAserver::receive(char *in_data, short &received,
        int &confirm_requested)
{
   CM_STATUS_RECEIVED status_received;
   CM_REQUEST_TO_SEND_RECEIVED rq_to_send_rcvd;
   CM_DATA_RECEIVED_TYPE what_received;
   CM_INT32 amount_rcvd;
   CM_RETURN_CODE rtn_code;
   int received_len = 0;
   amount_rcvd = 0;
   cmrcv(resource, (unsigned char *) in_data, &allowed_length,
&what_received,
       &amount_rcvd, &status_received, &rq_to_send_rcvd, &rtn_code);
   if(rtn_code != 0 )
     printf("return code from cmrcv is %d\n", rtn_code);
   received_len = amount_rcvd;
     if(amount_rcvd > 0)
     convert_ebcdic_to_ascii_field((unsigned char *) in_data,
received_len);
     in_data[received_len] = '\n';
     in_data[received_len + 1 ] = 1'\0';
     if(amount_rcvd > 0)
     if(what_received = = 2)
       received = 2;
     if(status_received = = CM_CONFIRM_SEND_RECEIVED)
       {
       confirm_requested = 1;
       received = SEND_IND;
     }
```

```
        if(status_received = = CM_SEND_RECEIVED)
          received = SEND_IND;
        if(status_received = = CM_CONFIRM_DEALLOC_RECEIVED)
          {
          confirm_requested = 1;
          received = SEND_IND;
          }
        if(status_received = = CM_DEALLOCATED_NORMAL)
          {
          confirm_requested = 0;
          received = SEND_IND;
          }
        if(rtn_code != 9)
          {
          if(rtn_code != OK)
            printf("error from receive and wait %d\n", rtn_code);
          }
        if(rtn_code != CM_OK)
          if(rtn_code != )CM_DEALLOCATED_NORMAL )
            rtn_code = 9;

        return(rtn_code);
} /* end SNA receive request */
```

The partner command to the send verb is the receive function. Because LU6.2 operates at the application layer as opposed to the transport layer (socket calls), the amount of data written at one time by the send command is the amount of data that is received by the receive command. With TCP socket calls, this is not the case. It is up to the application to determine a protocol boundary for the data. The amount of data written by a given socket is not necessarily the amount read. The status_received variable holds such indicators for the conversation as:

1. The partner has sent a request for a confirm.

2. The partner has requested a change in the conversation.

3. The partner has deallocated the conversation, and the partner has requested a confirm before the deallocation actually occurs.

In addition to receiving user data, the receive command is also used to determine the state of the conversation, or, more precisely, the status of the partner program.

The class handles most of these conditions for the user. The user need only check if a confirm has been requested, then call the SNA_Issue_confirm discussed below. And make sure the status of the conversation is nothing other than a 2. With any other status, the conversation is in a send or deallocated state.

```
int cSNAserver::SNA_Issue_confirm()
{
```

```
cmcfmd (sbco.resource,
    &sbco.rtn_code);
if(sbco.rtn_code != 0)
printf("error from confirm = %d\n",sbco.rtn_code);
return (sbco.rtn_code);
}
```

This command is issued in response to a confirm request from the partner returned by the receive verb.

```
int cSNAserver::disconnect()
{
CM_RETURN_CODE rtn_code;
if(!strlen((char *)MainFrameProfileName)) return 0;
cmdeal(resource, &rtn_code);
if(rtn_code != OK)
printf("error from m_deallocate %d\n ", rtn_code);
memset(MainFrameProfileName, 0, sizeof MainFrameProfileName);
return(rtn_code);
} /* end SNA_comm_disconnect */
```

This command deallocates the conversation and frees any allocated resources for further use. It is similar in function to the destructor command but is explicit to network resources.

```
void
cSNAserver::convert_ascii_to_ebcdic_field (
    unsigned char   * ascii_field,
    const unsigned int field_size)
{
    unsigned int i;
    assert(ascii_field != NULL);
    for (i = 0; i < field_size; i++) {
        ascii_field[i] =
            ascii_to_ebcdic_table[(unsigned)ascii_field[i]];
    }
}
void
cSNAserver::convert_ebcdic_to_ascii_field(
    unsigned char * ebcdic_field,
    const unsigned int field_size)
{
    unsigned int i;
    assert(ebcdic_field != NULL);
    for (i = 0; i < field_size; i++){
        ebcdic_field[i] =
            ebcdic_to_ascii_table[(unsigned)ebcdic_field[i]];
    }
}
```

13

UNIX Clients

The following example implements a client using cClient class (see Fig. 13.1). This example program, Con-client.cpp, simply connects to some configurable number of hosts and services. It generates a data string and gets a response back. It is built from the cClient class, which is presented next (see Fig. 13.2).

Figure 13.1
Clients and their relationship to communications programming.

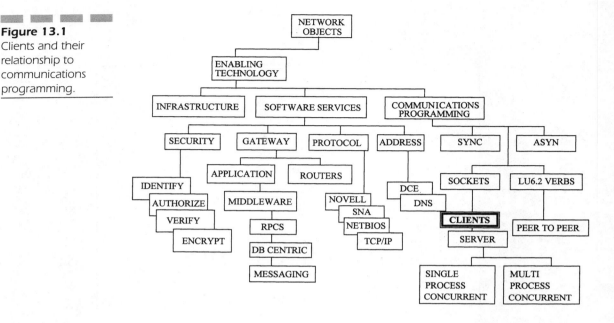

Figure 13.2
Defined classes for TCP/IP SNA client server communications.

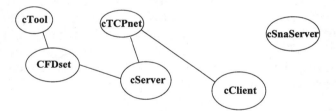

Conclient.cpp

```cpp
#include <sys/types.h>
#include "ctcpnet.hpp"
#include "errexit.hpp"
#include "cclient.hpp"
#include <iostream.h>
#include <stdio.h>

extern int errno;

#define BUFSIZE   4096
#define CCOUNT 64*1024 /* default character count */

#define USAGE "usage: Concurrent client [ -c count host1 host2…\n"
char service[12];
char hosts[12];
char conclient[] = "conclient";
char *retbuf;
```

```
int main ( int argc, char *argv[])

{
cClient client(conclient);
    int ccount = CCOUNT;
    int i, fd;
int no_hosts = 0;
    for (i = 1; i<argc; ++i) {
        if(strcmp (argv[i], "-s") == 0){
            i = i + 1;
            strcpy(service,argv[i] );
            i = i + 1;
        }
        if (strcmp ( argv[i], "-c") == 0 ) {
                if(++i<argc && (ccount = atoi(argv[1])))
                    continue;
                errexit(USAGE);
        }

        /* else a host */
    printf("service = %s\n", service);

    strcpy(hosts,argv[i] );
    printf ("argv[i] = %s and i = %d\n",argv[i],i);
    printf ("hostname = %s\n",hosts);
        fd = client.allocSocket(hosts,service);
    printf ("returning from allocSocket\n");
    printf ("socket fd = %d\n",fd);
    no_hosts = no_hosts + 1;
        }
while (1) }
char send_buf[80];
int retbuf_len;
cout <<'\n'<<"enter send string:";
cin >>send_buf;

client.sendTCP(send_buf,strlen(send_buf));
cout<<"record sent\n";
retbuf = new char[strlen((send_buf) + 1)];
retbuf_len = strlen(send_buf);

retbuf = client.receiveTCP();
cout <<'\n'<< retbuf;

}
delete []retbuf;
}
```

In the program above, a client object is created and used to provide the client connection to a service. The statements below, extracted from the program, show the calls required to provide the client communications.

- ▪ *cClient client(conclient);*: First, an object type is declared as cClient type with this statement.

- ▪ *fd = client.allocSocket(hosts,service);*: Next, the communication resources are allocated. The parameters *hosts* and *service* are passed and provide the name of the host to which the client is connecting

and the name of the service to which the client is connecting.
These variables are known to the programmer at startup time. In
this example they are provided at runtime.

■ *client.sendTCP(send_buf,strlen(send_buf));*. This statement is used to
send a request to the server application defined above. The parameters here are obvious.

■ *retbuf = client.receiveTCP();*. This routine is used to receive from the
server responses to the request sent in the routine above.

This listing shows the CCLIENT class used to implement the example
above.

```
#include "cclient.hpp"
#include "ctool.hpp"
#include <arpa/inet.h>
/********************************************************/
/*      Name: cclient.cpp                               */
/********************************************************/
#include "errexit.hpp"

cClient::cClient(char *name)
{
        strcpy(cli_name, name);
}
```

This is the constructor routine. It receives the name of the client and
copies it into the variable cli_name. It is not used for anything in this
example, but it could be logged for debugging and system tracking as
required.

```
int cClient::allocSocket(char *hosts, char *service)
{
    int    fdes, i;
    struct servent *pservEnt;
    struct protoent *pprotEnt;
    struct hostent *phostEnt;

    bzero((char *)&sin, sizeof (sin));
    sin.sin_family = AF_INET;

    //Service name to portnumber
    if ( pservEnt = getservbyname(service, pProt))
            sin.sin_port = pservEnt->s_port;
    else if (( sin.sin_port = htons((u_short) atoi(service))) = = 0)
            errexit(" unable to get protocol entry\n");
printf("service found \n");
cout <<"in cclient hosts = "<<hosts<<endl;
    //hostname to IP addr
    if ( phostEnt = gethostbyname(hosts))
      bcopy (phostEnt->h_addr, (char *)&sin.sin_addr,
                        phostEnt->h_length);
```

```
            else if (( sin.sin_addr.s_addr = inet_addr(hosts)) = =
INADDR_NONE
                errexit("unable to get host entry\n");
        printf ("host found\n");

        sockDesc = socket(PF_INET, SOCK_STREAM,0);
        if (sockDesc < 0)
                errexit("Unable to open socket\n");
        printf ("socket bound\n");
        if (connect (sockDesc, (struct sockaddr *)&sin,
            sizeof(sin)) <0)
            errexit("can't connect\n");
    printf ("connect done\n");
    if (ioctl (sockDesc, FIONBIO, (char *)&one))
            errexit ("cant markd socket nonblocking: %s\n",
                    sys_errlist[errno]);
        if (sockDesc > maxfd )
                maxfd = sockDesc;
        ++hcount;
        //FD_SET(fd, &afds);
        afds.FDset(sockDesc);
        maxfd = maxfd + 1;
            return sockDesc;
    }
```

The allocSocket routine shown above is the most complicated to understand, yet it is the most cookbook of the routines. It follows the socket protocol to get the destination address (host address), the service on the host to which the client is connecting, and the protocol used by the connection. The series of code below accomplishes this.

These data types are defined to provide the data structure used to establish the connection. Notice that each of these structures is populated by a different routine.

```
    struct servent *pservEnt;
    struct protoent *pprotEnt;
    struct hostnet *phostEnt;

    bzero((char *)&sin, sizeof (sin));
    sin.sin_family = AF_INET;

    //Service name to portnumber
    if (pservEnt = getservbyname(service, pProt))
            sin.sin_port = pservEnt->s_port;
        else if (( sin.sin_port = htons((u_short) atoi(service))) = = 0)
                errexit(" unable to get protocol entry\n");
printf ("service found\n");
    Cout <<" in cclient hosts = "<<hosts<<endl ;
        //hostname to IP addr
        if ( phostEnt = gethostbyname(hosts))
            bcopy (phostEnt->h_addr, (char *)&sin.sin_addr,
                            phostEnt->h_length);
        else if (( sin.sin_addr.s_addr = inet_addr(hosts)) = =
INADDR_NONE)
            errexit("unable to get host entry\n");
```

```
printf("host found\n");
Notice also in this the use of
sin.sin_port = htons((u_short) atoi(service))) == 0)
```

This code is used to translate the character notation of the port number into the proper network format for the port number.

Once the description is set up with the destination address, a socket or network connection is bound which includes the local address of the client, the local port number the client is using, the remote address of the client, and the remote port number of the service.

```
sockDesc = socket(PF_INET, SOCK_STREAM,0);
    if ( sockDesc < 0)
            errexit("Unable to open socket\n");
    printf("socket bound\n");
```

Using the addresses previously assigned and the socket number returned by the socket call, a connection to the remote address is attempted via the connect call.

```
if (connect (sockDesc, (struct sockaddr *)&sin, sizeof(sin)) <0)
```

The socket I/O becomes asynchronous through the ioctl call below:

```
if (ioctl (sockDesc, FIONBIO, (char *)&one))
```

Finally, this class uses the FDset class to set the socket descriptor as enabled.

```
afds.FDset(sockDesc);
```

Once the connection between the client and the server has occurred, data can flow between the two platforms. First, the sendTCP client is used to send data to the currently defined connection. In this implementation, the select command is used to determine whether a particular socket is read for output. The select command provides for three tests with each parameter:

```
if (select(maxfd, (fd_set*)0, wfds, (fd_set*)0,
(struct timeval *)0) <0)
```

The first parameter is the number of file descriptors (fds) to be tested. The second, third, and fourth parameters test fds for read, write, and error codes. The last parameter can be used to set for blocking time. But in this case, the blocking is set to zero or immediate return.

```
void cClient::sendTCP(char* buf, int buf_len)
{
    char rec_len[] = "0000";
    int fd, i;
if (buf_len = = 0) {
    for (i = 0; i<80; ++i)
        buf[i] = 'D';
}
    bcopy(&afds, &wcfds, sizeof(wcfds));
    (void ) ctool.mstime ((long *)0);/* set the epoch */
    bcopy(&wcfds, &wfds, sizeof(wfds));
    if (select(maxfd, (fd_set *)0, wfds, (fd_set *) 0,
            (struct timeval *)0) < 0)
        errexit("Select failed\n");
        for (fd = 0; fd < maxfd; ++fd){
        printf ("fd = %d, maxfd = %d\n",fd, maxfd);
        if (wfds.isFDready(fd))
        {
            int cc;
            printf ("write fd = %d\n",fd);
                printf ("write = %s\n", buf);
            cc = strlen(buf);
            sprintf(rec_len,"%4.4d",cc);
            printf ("buf length = %s\n", rec_len);
            cc = write(fd, rec_len, 4);
                cc = write(fd, buf, strlen(buf));
                            if ( cc < 0)
            errexit("error in write\n");
        }
    }
}
printf ("returning to main\n");
return ;
}
```

Because TCP protocol is streams, no record format is kept between the receiving and sending application. Therefore, some mechanism is needed to differentiate an application protocol. This one assumes that the client application will send a complete record to the TCPsend class on one call. The class then calculates the length of that record and places it in the beginning of the next buffer sent to the server.

```
cc = strlen(buf);
    sprintf(rec_len,"%4.4d",cc);
    printf("buf length = %s\n",rec_len);
    cc = write(fd,rec_len,4);
        cc = write(fd, buf, strlen(buf));
```

The server then reads the length and does a subsequent read to get all the data due it. Once this is complete, the receiving application has received all the data. This must be implemented between the sending and receiving classes, so that a sendTCP buffer always equals a receive TCP buffer.

Just like the sendTCP routine, the receiveTCP routine tests for availability of a read using the select call.

```
char* cServer::cReceive(int *active_conn)
{
char client_ip[80];
struct sockaddr_in    cli_addr;
       int fd, buf_len,clilen, client_port,gpn;
       //struct Services table[5];
    char message_size[5];
       bcopy (afds, rfds, sizeof(rfds));
       cout << "calling select/receive" << endl ;
               fd = *active_conn;

       clilen = sizeof(cli_addr);
    gpn = getpeername(fd, (struct sockaddr *) &cli_addr,&clilen);
          if (gpn < 0 ) {
             printf ("get peername failed %d\n",gpn );
             }
             else
             {
sprintf(client_ip,"client addr = %s\n",
    inet_ntoa(cli_addr.sin_addr));
//sprintf(client_port,"client addr = %d\n", cli_addr.sin_port);
    cout <<"clip = "<< client_ip << "clport = "<<ntohs(
cli_addr.sin_port)<<"fd = "<<fd<<endl;
                  }

    // gpn = getsockname(fd, (struct sockaddr *) &cli_addr,&clilen);
    // cout << "return from getsockname"<<cli_addr <<endl;

            if (select(nfds, rfds, (fd_set *)0,
                     (fd_set *) 0, (struct timeval *) 0) <0)
                errexit("select failed\n");
    cout << "returning for select/receive" << endl;
          for (fd = 0; fd < nfds; ++fd){
                 if(fd != sockDesc && rfds.isFDready(fd)){
             int byRead;
             cout <<"read ready fd = " <<fd<< endl;
             long now;
             byRead = read(fd,message_size 4);
             buf_len = atoi(message_size);
             cout <<"buflen = "<<buf_len;
             delete [] buf;
             buf = new char[buf_len + 1];
             byRead = read(fd, buf, buf_len);
             if (byRead < 0)
                errexit("error in reading\n");
             if(buf_len == 0){
                afds.FDclear (fd );
                close (fd);
             {
             // printf ("read = %s\n",buf);
               (void) ctool.mstime(&now);
               printf ("time %d\n",now);
//             afds.FDclear(fd);
               *active_conn = fd;
               cout <<"active conn return = "<<active_conn << endl ;
               buf[buf_len] = NULL;
```

```
                       return buf;
                       }
              }
       }
```

This part of the code reads the incoming message, looking for the first 4 bytes, which give the length of the rest of the message. It then uses these 4 bytes to read the rest of the message before returning it to the application.

```
byRead = read(fd,message_size,4);
              buf_len = atoi(message_size);
              cout <<"buflen = "<<buf_len;
              delete [] buf;
              buf = new char[buf_len + 1];
              byRead = read(fd, buf, buf_len);
if (buf_len = = 0)
              {
              afds.FDclear (fd );
              close (fd);
              }
```

Once the client has received all the information from the server, the afds set is cleared and the connection to the server is closed. The code above illustrates this.

The next set of code builds a single-process concurrent server, using the C++ wrappers discussed in Chap. 12. The application is a simple server application which uses the cServer class to simply echo the responses back to the client presented in the section above.

Query.hpp

```
#ifndef__QUERY_H
#define__QUERY_H
#include "cfdset.hpp"
#include "cserver.hpp"
#include "cclient.hpp"
#include <time.h>

#define BUFSIZ 4096

extern int errno;

int      servcies_no;
int      maxfd;

struct reqFrame{
              int    clientID;
              int    qLen;
              time_t time; //time_t is long
```

```
                     int     statFlag;
                     char    msgBuf[BUFSIZ];
                     };

                     //struct reqFrame mesg;
                     typedef reqFrame mesg;

                     int msgReceive(int fd, mesg *msgptr);
                     int msgReply(int fd, mesg *msgptr)

          #endif //__QUERY_H
```

Qserver.cpp

```cpp
          #include <sys/types.h>
          #include <iostream.h>
          //#include <stdio.h>
          #include "query.hpp"
          #define BUFSIZE 4096

          char *buf;

          int
          main (int argc, char *argv[])
          {
          int sock;
          printf ("initializing cServer object\n");
          cout <<"initializing cServer object" << endl;
          printf ("returning from cout call\n");
          cServer queryServ("queryServ", 1,5,"tcp");

          int msock, fd,ssock ;
          cout << "calling allocSocket\n";

          msock = queryServ.allocSocket();

          cout <<"socket allocated = "<< msock << endl ;
          while (1){
          cout <<"calling serverportready "<< endl ;
          sock = queryServ.cServerProtReady(msock);
          cout <<"sock from qserver.cServerProtReady = "<<sock <<endl ;
          if (sock > 0)
                  ssock = sock ;
                  cout << "calling cReceive" << endl ;
                  buf = queryServ.cReceive(&ssock);
                  cout <<"buf = "<<buf << endl ;
                  if (strlen(buf) > 0)
                  queryServ.sendTCP( buf,strlen(buf),ssock);
                  }
          }
```

Listed below are the four statements used by this program to implement the communications server piece for this application. Using the
cServer class presented in Chap. 12, the constructor receives the name of

the application server, the status flag used by the class internally, the length of the connection queue, and the protocol used by this server application.

```
cServer queryServ("queryServ",1,5,"tcp");
```

The next statement sets up the server to listen on the well-known port described in the services file.

```
msock = queryServ.allocSocket();
```

The next two statements do the receive from the client. Since the server is designed only to return what is sent, the next statement issued after the receive is the send. There is no need for a termination, as it runs forever.

```
buf = queryServ.cReceive(&ssock);
queryServ.sendTCP( buf,strlen(buf),ssock);
```

14

Multiprocess Concurrent Server

This chapter illustrates software designed to handle three different cases of proxy requirements using a C implementation of a multiprocess model (see Fig. 14.1). As Fig. 14.2 shows, there are three proxy services running on the gateway from which users request information. These services include the ability to request via TCP/IP clients data residing in CICS mainframe regions, "SNA CICS proxy"; data residing on MVS systems (not necessarily CICS), "SNA file transfer proxy"; and data residing elsewhere on the TCP/IP corporate LAN, the "TCP/IP proxy."

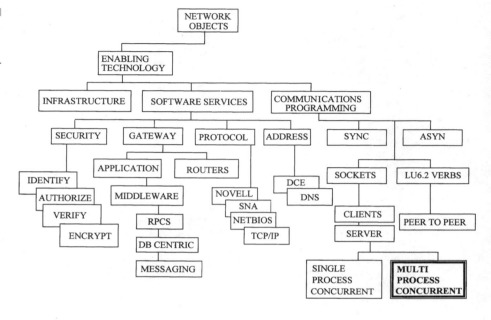

Figure 14.1

SNA_TCP_smo.c architecture.

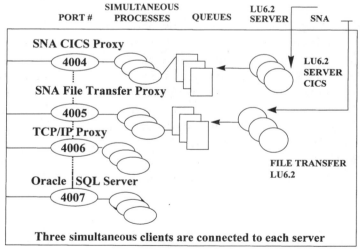

Figure 14.2

Process configuration on RS6000 server.

Each of these services is implemented as a multiprocess concurrent service. A single-process concurrent server was not used because the length of the response and the amount of data requested by each transaction was so long that separate processes were viable options. As can be seen from the diagram, the services are running on a particular port to which the client connects. Once the connection is accepted, the server forks, creating a separate process. The forked process then sends out the data to the back-end system, either SNA or TCP/IP. The process then waits on a message queue for the response from the SNA service. Once the response is received, the process returns the data to the client originating the request. All the SNA services work this way. The TCP/IP proxy server simply forwards the request to the appropriate service and waits for a reply (synchronously) from the service. Once the reply is received, the data is returned to the client as it is received on the gateway from the back-end service.

The Oracle SQL server residing on the gateway is nothing more than a transparent routing mechanism for Oracle SQL requests originating at the client network. As the client network is Netbios, there is another gateway that translates Netbios to TCP/IP and then to the gateway. The gateway then forwards the request to the appropriate back-end Oracle server.

Figure 14.3 shows the general construction of the SNA_TCP_smo.c proxy service. Notice that at runtime there are at least four different input choices used when starting the particular service and five different output choices. This enables a single program to be used to provide multiple proxy services and to provide a testing and debugging mechanism (program generated).

Figure 14.4 shows the conversation protocol used to send requests to SNA systems. When a request comes in from the client, the server forks, and the SNA connection is initiated. Then an SNA connect request is sent over the connection to cause the partner conversation to occur (m_allocate). Once the connection has been made, the send is issued via SNA_send, and an M_confirm and a deallocate end that conversation.

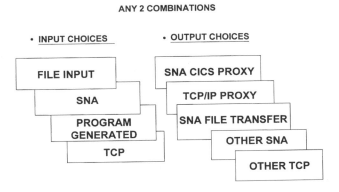

Figure 14.3
Gateway communications software, SNA_TCP_smo.c proxy service.

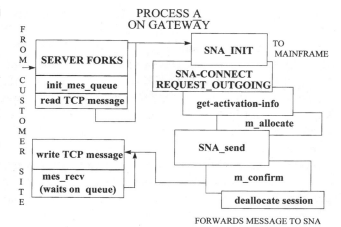

Once that happens, the process writes a message to the client confirming that the request has been delivered, and the process waits on a message queue for the response from the SNA or back-end system.

A second process (same program) is initialized as SNA in and TCP out (see Fig. 14.5) and is executed from the mainframe when the request previously sent is complete. This gateway service then receives the request and, based on the transaction, determines the message queue to be written to, the same one the other process is waiting on. The SNA/TCP/OUT program then reads from SNA and writes to the message queue until all the records have been delivered. Likewise, the process above, waiting on the message queue, begins to return the records to the requester after the first record is received.

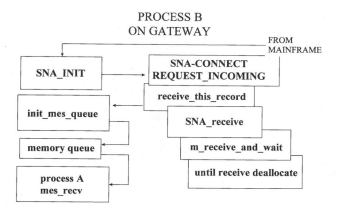

Figure 14.6

SNA_TCP_smo.c TCP in–to–TCP out conversation protocol.

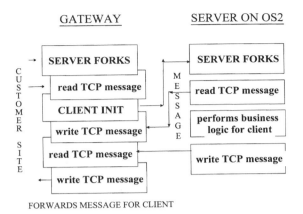

The TCP in to TCP out process is a similar, synchronous design (see Fig. 14.6). The server still forks a new request on a connect request from the client, reads the message, and becomes a client to the TCP back-end service. The back-end service then performs whatever function is required and returns the results over the listening TCP/IP client. The forked proxy service then reads each request from the back-end service and writes it out to the requesting client.

The file transfer service for SNA, not shown, uses a product called Network Data Mover (NDM), an LU6.2 service, that starts file transfer jobs on the mainframe from a requesting TCP/IP client. The client then waits for the file to arrive from the mainframe onto the gateway. Once the proxy service recognizes that the file has arrived, it returns the contents to the waiting client.

Components of SNA_TCP_smo.c

Now that an overview of the specific services provided by the gateway has been given, this chapter describes the runtime parameters or attributes which define the different invocations of the program for a particular service.

The chapter presents the SNA_TCP_smo.c code for those who may be interested. It is implemented as a multiprocess concurrent server and utilizes the fork() system call to create another instance of the process after each separate client connection.

Runtime Attributes for SNA_TCP_smo.c Processes

In this example, three processes are started using the same load module to handle connections from TCP clients to:

- CICS systems using transaction-based requests
- SNA systems using file transfer between the mainframe and the UNIX gateway
- Other TCP-based services

For example, there are three command files: (1) allocsna, (2) allocndm, and (3) allocnet.

1. *allocsna.* Shown below is the example file for allocsna which starts the CICS SNA service for TCP/IP clients. This command file executes the program SNA_TCP_smo and provides it with a number of parameters for runtime initialization. These runtime parameters describe, among other things, the input for the service, the output, and the port number on the network to use for the service. In this instance, the input is TCP network and the output is SNA network (-i and -o parameters). The port number on which to publish this service is 4003. No output other than SNA is required for the service, such as an additional TCP service; had it been, it would be described with a -P parameter. An example of this is shown in the next two command start-up procedures.

```
/SNA_TCP_smo -l 101 -s 0 -d 2 -t 1 -f/u/billyarb/config.test\
i TCP -o SNA -c 1 -p 4003
```

2. *allocndm.* This command file is used to start the NDM service to provide a file transfer mechanism to and from the mainframe. As can be seen from the parameters, the same program, SNA_TCP_smo, is executed. This time, however, it is initialized with TCP for input and NDM for output. Remember, NDM is the requesting vehicle for getting data from the mainframe. This time the TCP network port number is 4004. Because this service writes the returning data to another server as well as to the returning client, the port number on which that service is running must be described to the program, and be known ahead of time. That port number in this case is 700, described by the input -P parameter.

```
./SNA_TCP_smo -1 101 -s 0 -d 2 -t 1 -f/u/billyarb/config.test\
i TCP -o NDM -c 1 -p 4004 -P 700
```

3. *allocnet.* The third service begins with the allocnet command file, once again starting the same program, SNA_TCP_smo. This time it is initialized with the same input parameter, TCP, since all client requests to this service are provided over a TCP network, but the output is also TCP. Remember, for the discussion above, that this client is accustomed to starting a TCP network service that passes the requests from a TCP client to another TCP server located in a Windows NT client. This time, the well-known port at which to listen for connections is located at 4005, and the server will request TCP service from another TCP server on port 700 (-P parameter).

```
./SNA_TCP_smo -1 101 -s 0 -d 2 -t 1 -f/u/billyarb/config.test\
i TCP -o TCP -c 1 -p 4005 -P 700
```

In addition to these four network configuration parameters (-i, -o, -p, and -P), there are other configuration or program features which can be set. These include -t, whether to keep the log files generated from each invocation of the service, and -f, a descriptive file containing network parameters. If the output is SNA, the -c parameter tells the program whether to ask for a confirm after each message sent. These are described below.

- *log file retention -t.* For each invocation of a given service by a client, a log file is produced whose name consists of the output parameter described in the -o parameter with the date and time the request was made appended to the name. For example, if a client requested NDM service for Chemlink data on 12-20-95 at 9:15 A.M., a log file would be produced by the program with the name NDM_12-20-95_9:15:33 (the 33 is seconds). Should an error occur, the log file will remain on file for review. Unless the -t parameter is 1, if all goes as expected, the log file will be deleted after the service completes. During testing of additional services and for debugging purposes, the log files can be retained by setting the -t parameter to 1. A word of warning: Things can get pretty crowded with log files in a busy system. Unless there is a reason to keep the logs, a 0, delete the files if all goes well, is recommended.

Test Parameters

During development of additional services, it may be useful to simulate network input with test parameters to the designated output. If this is required, the -l, -s, and -i parameters are configured to read a test file of the user's choice and write that data to an output service—SNA, NDM, TCP, or a future enhancement. It is not anticipated that this feature will be used except by developers making changes to the code for problem determination or functional enhancement.

- # 1 = Number of program-generated test data messages to send.
- # s = Length of test data string generated by the program (0 when data is not generated).
- # d = Direction; 2 will put test data across the network and back.
- # t = Keep log files; 1 = true, 0 = false.
- # f = The input file name of the network parameters.
- # i = Input source. TCP is input from the network. Test data is input from a file. Use a fully qualified file name.
- # o = System destination: TCP, NDM, SNA.
- # c = Confirm; for 1, ask for confirm after each send.
- # P = Port number of additional services needed by this service.

This concludes the runtime documentation and the parameters used to distinguish the service provided by one process from that provided by other processes.

SNA Peer Server

As described above for the SNA CICS service, there is not only a TCP client input, but also an SNA server component on the RS6000. As depicted in the overview documentation for this service, this program gets invoked by the CICS transaction that is returning the data requested by the originating TCP transaction. Recall that the originating transaction is waiting on a message queue for the requested mainframe service to complete and return the results to the gateway. Once the CICS transaction has completed the request, the SNA_TCP_in run module is executed as a peer program by the CICS transaction on the RS6000 to return the data to the client waiting for it at the specific message queue.

Additionally, this transaction is used when data is pushed to the RS6000, as in the COB data transactions described above.

This transaction is configured like all the others and uses the same programs, except that it is compiled into a different runtime module by the make file (described next) as SNA_TCP_in. The input -i parameters are coded as SNA to describe the input, and the output for this module is TERM to indicate that it is sent to a message queue determined by the transaction requested. Shown below is the runtime configuration used to invoke this SNA peer server.

```
./SNA_TCP_in -l 101 -s 0 -d 2 -t 1 -f/u/billyarb/config.test\
-i SNA -o TERM
```

Make Files

Like all C programs, this is composed of subroutines. Many of these routines are located in the SNA_TCP_smo.c program itself; others are located in different C files. Below is a list of the different files that contain many of the programs used by the SNA_TCP_smo.c gateway. They are described briefly here, but the source code is presented in far more detail later in this chapter.

- SRC1 = SNA_TCP_smo.c
- SRC2 = SNA_interface.c
- SRC3 = common_routines.c
- SRC4 = tcp_client_lib.c
- SRC5 = a2e.c
- SRC6 = messqueu.c
- SRC7 = Getsnafiles.c

- *SNA_TCP_smo.c.* This program contains the main subroutine. The other program files contain subroutines called by this program. In addition, this program contains other subroutines local to this program.
- *SNA_interface.c.* This program contains subroutine interfaces for all SNA LU6.2 interfaces. This file can be modified to use other LU6.2 routines without changes to the calling code. For example, the calling code uses four routines: SNA_Connect, SNA_send, SNA_receive, and SNA_Disconnect. Each of these subroutines gets translated into the appropriate SNA calls used by the existing interface. Currently,

the SNA_interface file supports RS6000 SNA Server and the UNIX AT&T LU6.2 product. The RS6000 is being used in this implementation. However, it can easily be modified to use other interfaces, such as the Sun RPC LU6.2 implementation.

- *common_routines.c.* This file contains the routines used by all the other routines. They include file open routines, read routines, file write routines, and file exists routines.

- *tcp_client_lib.c.* Similar to the SNA_interface routines, this file contains socket-level routines for client and server interfaces. For example, socket setup and socket read and write routines are contained here and allow the user program to use higher-level application calls while having little knowledge about the underlying socket protocols.

- *messqueu.c.* Like the other C files, this one contains routines designed to manage the message queue deployed in the main program.

- *Getsnafiles.c.* This uses the C interface for the Network Data Mover (NDM). These routines are used to connect and send requests for file transfer to the Chemlink mainframe. They are initiated when the TCP client requests intraday data from the Chemlink system.

- *a2e.c.* This call is used to translate ascii characters on UNIX to ebcdic for the mainframe.

The make file is used to compile and link the SNA_TCP_smo.c source code and includes other C files that contain subroutines needed, the main code, and the libraries required by other subroutines.

```
    MAKE = make CC = "$(CC)" AS = "$(AS)" LD = "$(LD)" AR = "$(AR)"
CPP = "$(CPP)"
    # compiler executables
    #CPP - C pre-processor
    #AR - Object archiver / librarian
    CPP = /lib/cpp
    AR = /bin/ar
    CC = cc
    #CC = gcc
    # The names of the targets. The command "make" can be used to
      make all
    # the targets. The command "make <target_name>" makes a
      particular target.
    # For example, the command "make exasync" will make the exasync
      target.
    TARGET1 = SNA_TCP_smo
    TARGET2 = read_socket
    TARGET3 = a2e
```

```
TARGET4 = write_file_record
TARGET5 = tcp_client_lib
TARGET6 = write_file
TARGET7 = messqueu
TARGETS = $(TARGET1)
# Where to get includes and libraries
INCPATH =
SYSLIBS = -lodm -lsrc -lcpic -liconv
# source and includes files
SRC1 = SNA_TCP_smo.c
SRC2 = SNA_interface.c
SRC3 = common_routines.c
SRC4 = tcp_client_lib.c
SRC5 = a2e.c
SRC6 = messqueu.c
OBJ1 = $(SRC1:.c = .o)
OBJ2 = $(SRC2:.c = .o)
OBJ3 = $(SRC3:.c = .o)
OBJ4 = $(SRC4:.c = .o)
OBJ5 = $(SRC5:.c = .o)
OBJ6 = $(SRC6:.c = .o)
GCCFLAGS = -ansi -pedantic -Wall -Wtraditional -Wshadow -
            Wpointer-arith -pipe
#CFLAGS = -g $(GCCFLAGS) $(INC) $(DEFS)
CFLAGS = -g $(INC) $(DEFS)
#LDFLAGS = Bstatic -pg
SABER_FLAGS = $(CFLAGS) -DXTFUNCPROTO -1$(INC)
LINK.c = $(CC) $(LDFLAGS)
all: $(TARGETS)
$(TARGET1): $(OBJ1) $(OBJ2) $(OBJ3) $(OBJ4) $(OBJ5) $(OBJ6)
    $(LINK.c) $(OBJ1) $(OBJ2) $(OBJ3) $(OBJ4) $(OBJ5) $(OBJ6)\
$(SYSLIBS) -o SNA_TCP_smo
clean:
    rm -f*.o *.In*.out
.PRECIOUS:$(TARGET1)
```

The following is a list of the routines used by SNA_TCP_smo.c:

```
/* Program Name: SNA_TCP_smo.c
main(argc,argv)
{
```

- *signal (SIGCLD, SIG_IGN);* A UNIX routine to tell forked children to exit without notifying the parent process. Otherwise the children become zombies and clog up system resources when they terminate.

- *process_args(argc,argv);* Reads the arguments provided in the runtime files discussed above.

- *set_args();* Sets the arguments for the SNA_TCP_IN load module.

- *determine_data_source();* Determines the source (network) of data input arguments provided in the runtime arguments.

- *do_processing (int newsockfd)*. Program forks to this routine when listen and accept detect a client connection to the server.
- *date_time(&this_run)*. Returns the date and time used to name the log file.
- *logf = open_file(log_file_name)*. Opens the log file for this process.
- *generate_test_data()*. Generates test data if it is selected as input.
- *log_transaction_data()*. Logs the data read by the transaction in 72-byte segments.
- *SNA_initialize_network(config_file_in)*. Reads the file designated by the config_file_in argument. For informational purposes only for CPIC interface.
- *sna_init(&usr_provided)*. Initializes the SNA connection to the SNA network.
- *SNA_Connect_request_incoming()*. Manages connections of incoming allocate requests from partner.
- *open_data_source(source_file_name)*. Opens the input data source specified in the runtime parameters.
- *start_time = time(0)*. Returns the time.
- *calc_data_rate()*. Calculates the data rate over the network.
- *data_available = readline (clsockfd, send_data,4000,0)*. Reads data from an open socket and returns the address.
- *clsockfd = f_client (srv_port)*. Opens a socket connection to a server.
- *F_str_cli (clsockfd, send_data)*. Writes data to an open socket.
- *return_ok = process_ndm()*. Processes the client's request for intraday Chemlink data.
- *return_ok = forward_client_request_to_sna()*. Forwards the client's request for GEOPAC data.
- *return_ok = sna_connect_error()*. Handles SNA connection errors.
- *delete_message_queue(messqueue_file)*. Deletes message queues being used by the process when they are no longer needed.
- *int more_to_send(int data_source)*. Reads data from an open data source until there is no more.
- *receive_this_record()*. Receives records from an SNA partner on the mainframe that has established a conversation.
- *int determine_trans_status()*. Determines whether the incoming response is a close of business originating from the mainframe or

is a response from the mainframe to a client request for data. If it is the former, the data is written to a file. If it is the latter, the data is stored in a message queue.

- *time_req = create_geo_file_name(geofilename,first_rec):* Builds a filename from the transaction request received by the TCP server and by the SNA receive program.

- *file_status = file_exists (geofilename):* Determines if a file exists and, if so, whether it contains data.

- *first_read = open_file(geofilename):* Opens the file named in geofilename.

- *message_q_id = assign_mess_queue_key (geofilename,proj):* Assigns a message queue ID based on the geofilename and a project ID. This message queue is used to coordinate the async conversation used by geopac.

- *int return_file_contents (int sockno , char "geofilename).* Returns a file named as geofilename to the open socket sockno.

- *read_len = readfile(geo,send_data,usr_provided.allowed_length).* Performs a low-level read on the file opened as geo and reads up to the allowed length, returning the address in send_data.

- *int determine_response_status().* Internal routine to determine if a file already exists for an existing query.

- *file_status = mess_queue_exists (geofilename):* Checks to see if the message queue initialized by init_mess_queue exists.

- *if (SNA_send(char &init_data,int do_confirm).* Sends data to a partner program that is already in conversation and determines whether to issue a confirm based on the value of do_confirm.

- *if (SNA_disconnect() = = 0).* Disconnects SNA conversation from the network.

- *connect_rc = SNA_Connect_request_outgoing():* Creates a connection to an SNA partner (allocates a conversation).

- *SNA_receive(rec_data , &issue_send,&issue_confirm):* Receives records from the SNA connection to GEOPAC.

- *messqueue_file = init_mess_queue(message_q_id):* Initializes a message queue that is identified by the message_q_id, which is produced from the geofilename,proj combination.

- *mes_rc = write_mess_queue(messqueue_file,rec_data):* Writes the data in rec_data to the messqueue_file initialized above.

- *SNA_Issue_confirm()*: Issues a confirm to requesting partners in an SNA LU6.2 conversation.

- *return_ok = Ret_F_str_cli (int newsockfd, char *return_transdata)*: Returns data to an open socket pointed to by return_transdata.

- *ret_len = mes_recv (int messqueue_file,char *mesg); /* mesgptr*/*. Reads a message from the message queue pointed to by messqueue_file and places the data in &mesg.

- *void delete_message_queue(messqueue_file)*: Deletes the message queue identified by messqueue_file.

- *process_ndm()*. Processes TCP client requests for intraday data to the Chemlink system via NDM file transfer.

- *void submit_ndm_request()*: Submits requests via NDM interface for intraday Chemlink data.

/* Program Name: SNA_TCP_smo.c */

```c
#include <stdio.h>
#include <sys/types.h>
#include <fcntl.h>
#include <string.h>
#include <time.h>
#include <sys/wait.h>
#include <signal.h>

#include "SNA_Usr_params.h"
#include "SNA_Constants.h"
#include "network_common_routines.h"
#include "inet.h"
#include "msgq.h"
#include "mesg.h"
#include "geo_hdr.h"

#define ISSUE_SEND_CMMD 0x005
#define DEBUG 1
#define FILE_INPUT 1
#define GENERATED 2
#define MAX_RETRYS 1
#define NETWORK 3
#define TCP 4
#define SNA 5
struct ret_date_time this_run;
int return_ok = 2;
int tran_status;
int intransient = 0;
int true = 1;
int loops = 0;
int loop = 0;
int size = 0;
```

```
int start_not_set = 1;
long time();
long start_time;
long stop_time;
long bps =  0;
long delta_time  = 0;
long bytes = 0;

int data_available = 1;
int i;
int zz;
int do_confirm = 0;
int rlength;
int send_only = 0;
int_issue_confirm = 0;
int connect_rc;
int sleep_time = 60;/* is default */
int data_source;
int retry_send = 0;
int i_rc = 0;
int number_messages = 0;
int ret_len = 1;
int message_queue_complete;

short issue_send-0;
char *send_data;
unsigned char *rec_data;
char return_transdata[512];
char rs_tp[] = "ATS1";
char closefile[] = "closefile\n";
char filename[] = "snatcp.log\n";
char geofilename[80];
char source_file_name[80];
char target_system[20];
char GEO_COB[] = "C";
struct SNA_params usr_provided ;
int sockfd;
int clsockfd;
long message_q_id = 0;
char proj = `S';
int messqueue_file;
int open_this_file = 1;
int first_read = 1;
int logf;
FILE *data_file_name;
int more_data = 1;

int newsockfd,clilen,childpid;
int time_req;
Mesg mesg;
GEO_TRAN *first_rec;
int trace_on;
int ignsigcld;

u_short tcp_port;
u_short srv_port;
main(argc,argv)

int argc;
char **argv;
{
```

```
struct  sockaddr_in  cli_addr, serv_addr;

pname = argv[0];

/*if (ignsigcld) { prevents zombie processes from children
signal (SIGCLD, SIG_IGN);
}
*/

signal (SIGCLD, SIG_IGN) ;

if (argc < 3 )
explain_args();
else
process_args(argc,argv);
/*
set_args();
*/

if (do_confirm = = 1)
printf ("confirm requested\n");
else
printf ("confirm not requested\n");

determine_data_source();

if (data_source = = TCP) {

printf ("data source detected TCP input forking\n");
/* open tcp socket */

if ( ( sockfd = socket (AF_INET, SOCK_STREAM, 0)) < 0)
    printf("server cannot open stream socket\n");

serv_addr.sin_family = AF_INET;
serv_addr.sin_addr.s_addr = hton(INADDR_ANY);
serv_addr.sin_port = htons(tcp_port);
if (bind(sockfd, (struct sockaddr *) &serv_addr, sizeof(serv_addr))
    < 0)
    printf ("server cannot bind to local address\n");
printf ("executing listen\n");
listen(sockfd, 5);

for (; ;) {
/* wait for a connection from a client process. */

    clilen = sizeof(cli_addr);
    newsockfd = accept(sockfd, (struct sockaddr *) &cli_addr,
                &clilen);
    if (newsockfd < 0 )
        printf ("server accept error\n");

    if ( ( childpid = form()) <0)
        printf ("server : fork error \n");

    else if (childpid = = 0 ) {
        close(sockfd) ;
        do_processing(newsockfd);
        /* str_echo (newsockfd);
        call the function to put it on the message queue */
        exit (0);
    }
```

```
            close(newsockfd);   /* parent process */
            }
    }
    else
    {
    do_processing (0);
    }
    }
    do_processing (int newsockfd){

    do {

    open_log_file();

    determine_data_source();

    if (open_this_file = = 0)
    setup_socket_rec_file();

    if (data_source = = GENERATED)
    {
        generate_test_data();
        log_transaction_data();
    }
    if (data_source = = SNA)
    {
    SNA_initialize_network(config_file_in);
    sna_init(&user_provided);
    printf ("calling SNA_Connect_request_incoming\n");
    SNA_Connect_request_incoming();
    free (rec_data);
    rec_data = (char *) malloc(usr_provided.allowed_length);
    printf ("returning from SNA_Connect_request_incoming\n");
    }
    if (data_source = = FILE_INPUT)
    {
        open_data_source(source_file_name);
    }
    if (data_source = = TCP)
        open_data_source(source_file_name);

    if (strcmp (target_system,"TCP") = = 0 )

    {
        /* simulate_SNA input to TCP */
            clsockfd = f_client(srv_port);
    #ifdef DEBUG
        sprintf (error_script," TCP init\n");
        bytes_written = log(logf,error_script,strlen(error_script));
    #endif
    more_to_send (data_source) ;
    #ifdef DEBUG
        sprintf (error_script,"data = \n");
        bytes_written = log(logf,error_script,strlen(error_script));
    #endif
            strcat(return_transdata,"OK\n");
        return_ok = Ret_F_str_cli ( newsockfd, return_transdata );
      if (start_not_set = = 1) {
      start_time = time(0);
```

```
      start_not_set = 0;
      }
  if (number_messages > 0 )
  calc_data_rate();
  number_messages = number_messages + 1;
  if ( clsockfd < 0 )
      {
      printf ("connection to server failed\n");
      sprintf (error_script,"socket connect error to NETSETL\n");
      bytes_written = log(logf,error_script,strlen(error_script));
        strncpy (send_data,"FAILED\n",7);
        Ret_F_str_cli (newsockfd, send_data);
      }
      else
      {
      printf ("writing data to netset server\n");
      F_str_cli (clsockfd, send_data);
      printf ("returning from netset server send\n");
      sprintf (error_script,"data request delivered to
      Netsetserver\n");
      bytes_written = log(logf,error_script,strlen(error_script));
      }
      /* while more to send */
      if (data_source = = TCP) {
         while (data_available > 0) {
            printf ("waiting for response from netset\n");
            data_available = readline (clsockfd, send_data,4000,0);
            printf ("response received from netset\n");
            printf ("d = %s\n",send_data);
            F_str_cli (newsockfd, send_data);
            }
      sprintf (error_script,"data returned from NTSET server
      request\n");
      bytes_written = log(logf,error_script,strlen(error_script));
      close(newsockfd);
      close (clsockfd);
      }
  } /* target system equals TCP */

  if (strcmp (target_system,"TERM") = = 0 )

  {
  #ifdef DEBUG
      sprintf (error_script,"ocos initialization ok rc = %d\n",i_rc);
      bytes_written = log(logf,error_script,strlen(error_script));
  #endif

  while (more_to_send (data_source) = = more_data )
  {

  }/* end while more to send */

  if (message_queue_complete = = 1) {
      if (trace_on = = 0) {
      unlink(log_file_name);
      }
  }

  }
  if (strcmp ( target_system, "NDM" ) = = 0 )
```

```
    {
            strcat(return_transdata,"OK\n");
            return_ok = Ret_F_str_cli ( newsockfd, return_transdata );
            clsockfd = f_client ( srv_port ); /* open netset server */
              if ( clsockfd < 0 )
                {
                  printf ("connection to server failed\n");
  sprintf (error_script,"socket connect error to NETSETL\n");
  bytes_written = log(logf,error_script,strlen(error_script));

            strncpy (send_data,"FAILED\n",7);
            Ret_F_str_cli (newsockfd, send_data);
            }
            else
            {
            printf ("writing data to netset server\n");
  sprintf (error_script,"writing CHEMLINK data to NETSETL\n");
  bytes_written = log(logf,error_script,strlen(error_script));
            F_str_cli (clsockfd, send_data);
            printf ("returning from netset server send\n");
            }

  return_ok = process_ndm();
  if (return_ok > 0 ) {
      if (trace_on == 0)
      unlink ( log_file_name);
      unlink ( geofilename);
      }
      else
      {
        sprintf( error_script, " file return failed \n");
        bytes_written = log(logf,error_script,strlen(error_script));
      }
    } /* if NDM OUTGOING */
    if (strcmp ( target_system, "SNA" ) == 0 )
    {

      SNA_initialize_network(config_file_in);
      /**********************************************************/
      /*This routine is used to initialize the SNA verb parameters
      with the parameters provided by the user at runtime, and read
      in by SNA_initialize_network.*/
      /**********************************************************/
      sna_init(&usr_provided);
      /**********************************************************/
      /*SNA_Connect_request_outgoing. This function requests that
      a conversation be allocated with the tp requested in the
      usr_provided.tpn parameter that resides in the CICS region
      designated by the usr_provided.luname over a mode included
      in the usr_provided.mode_name.*/
      /**********************************************************/
      connect_rc = SNA_Connect_request_outgoing();
      #ifdef DEBUG
      sprintf(error_script,"return code from connect-request = %d\n
",connect_rc);
      bytes_written = log(logf,error_script,strlen(error_script));
      #endif
      if (connect_rc == 0)
      {
```

```
        return_ok = forward_client_request_to_sna();

        } /* if connect_rec = 0 */
        else

        {
        return_ok = sna_connect_error();

        } /* connect request not equal zero */


        if (return_ok > 0) {
            unlink ( geofilename);
        if (trace_on == 0) {
            unlink ( log_file_name);
            sprintf (error_script," response delivered file deleted
%s\n",geofilename);
            bytes_written = log(logf,error_script,strlen(error_script));
            }
        }
        else
        {
        if (time_req == 1) {
            unlink (geofilename);
            if (trace_on == 0)
            unlink ( log_file_name);
        }
    }

    close (first_rec);
    close (newsockfd);
    delete_message_queue(messqueue_file);

    } /* for target = SNA */

    free(send_data);
    free(rec_data);
    true = 0;
    exit(0);

    } while (true == 1);
    }/* do processing */
```

INDEX

About the Author

William Yarborough is a communications software engineer and network architect with over 18 years of experience in all facets of the software system life cycle, including 10 years specializing in network architecture, systems integration, and client/server systems development. He is currently consulting to a number of Fortune 500 companies on infrastructure development to support network integration and client/server connectivity across multiple platforms and network topologies.